GW00726724

DISCOVERING JESUS IN THE OTHER

DISCOVERING JESUS *in the* OTHER

Challenging the Myth of Otherness

Alan Abernethy
and Jim Deeds

VERITAS

Published 2024 by
Veritas Publications
7–8 Lower Abbey Street
Dublin 1
Ireland
publications@veritas.ie
www.veritas.ie

ISBN 978 1 80097 078 6

Copyright © Alan Abernethy and Jim Deeds, 2024

10 9 8 7 6 5 4 3 2 1

The material in this publication is protected by copyright law. Except as may be permitted by law, no part of the material may be reproduced (including by storage in a retrieval system) or transmitted in any form or by any means, adapted, rented or lent without the written permission of the copyright owners. Applications for permissions should be addressed to the publisher.

A catalogue record for this book is available from the British Library.

Cover designed by Clare Meredith, Veritas Publications
Typeset by Padraig McCormack, Veritas Publications
Printed in the Republic of Ireland by SPRINT-print Ltd, Dublin

Veritas Publications is a member of Children's Books Ireland and Publishing Ireland.

Veritas books are printed on paper made from the wood pulp of managed forests. For every tree felled, at least one tree is planted, thereby renewing natural resources.

Contents

Introduction

On a warm evening in April 2021, Jim Deeds was launching one of his books in Clonard Monastery, just off the Falls Road in Belfast. Having been friends for many years up to that point, Jim invited Alan Abernethy to be there to share this moment with him. Alan gladly accepted and returned to Clonard, a place where he had prayed, met with friends and attended meetings over the years. At the end of the book launch, Alan came up to Jim and, giving him a congratulatory hug, whispered in his ear, 'You and I are going to write a book, brother.' Jim looked at Alan and saw an excited glint in his eye. Captured by his enthusiasm, Jim simply replied, 'Okay, let's do it!'

What ensued was many meetings, usually including a walk in places that meant something to us on our faith journey. We walked up the Falls Road and down the Shankill. We prayed in Clonard Monastery and St Anne's Cathedral. We drank cups of coffee and listened to each other. And in that listening, we listened for the nudges of the Holy Spirit. This book is, we believe, a product of some of those nudges.

The reflections herein are borne out of our very different and yet at the same time very similar experiences of growing up and living through the period in our history known as 'The Troubles' – a strange title for a bewildering period of mayhem, murder, confusion and mistrust. There is no doubt our experiences impacted upon us and helped shape us in multiple ways. At the centre of our journeys is a faith that struggled and wavered. However, it also challenged, inspired and changed us.

As we penned these thoughts it became increasingly obvious that we were both helped along the way by the many saints or angels who have appeared in various guises to help us on our journey of faith. There were those who made us question and even doubt what denominational faith stood for, but that was an important part of us owning our own journey. Family and friends are key to our stories and we are forever grateful for how they have loved and shaped us, showing us the loveliness of Jesus. We want to honour all of them, even if we can only mention a few by name in these pages.

The idea for this book came from a friendship that grew and developed as we shared events and interactions. We have been challenged and enriched by each other's life stories as they reveal the need to understand our history from the perspective of someone from the 'other side' of the community. In a world where we so often demonise the other, we have been challenged and inspired to discover Jesus in the other.

This journey of discovery is so often not even embarked upon because of prejudice, misunderstanding and myth. If we are secure in the Jesus we follow, there is no need to fear the other, but rather it is a joy to discover Jesus in the other. As part of our journey in writing we have walked together through the streets that appear in our stories. We have visited each other's homes and places of worship. This journey has brought us joy and inspiration. We have been blessed by each other and by the one we seek to follow.

The stories we tell are in one way typical Belfast stories, replete with tears of sadness and tears of joy and humour. In another way, we have found that our particular stories are part of the universal story of seeking purpose, peace and hope in the midst of the messiness of life.

Our prayer is that you will find hope, joy and peace as you read our reflections. We also pray that it will disturb, inspire and encourage you to discover Jesus in the other. Finally, when all is said and done, we believe that there is 'one Lord, one faith and one baptism' (Eph 4:5). May you experience this oneness as you read our book.

CHAPTER ONE

Roots, Culture and Conflict

ALAN > Who Am I?

I was born a 'Protestant', and I grew up in the beautiful and yet torturous city of Belfast. Religious labels in Northern Ireland can be unhelpful and divisive. I have always found it difficult to hear the terms Catholic and Protestant used when describing the terrible divisions within this place I love and call home.

The religious labels of Protestant or Catholic are often associated with the political preferences of unionist or republican. These overlaps are often correct, but they distort the picture for the many people in this place who seek to live out their faith. They also fail to recognise and understand the many people who have discarded any public or private declaration of faith. The truth is that there are countless people in Northern Ireland who have been sickened by a religious language and practice that can be sectarian, excluding and divisive.

As someone who has served in one of the main denominations on this island, I have to recognise that the churches have been part of the problem. We have stubbornly refused to change and have at times been unable or unwilling to discern the gentle whisper of God. However, I also want to affirm the many people who have sought to be peacemakers and have discovered Jesus in the other: 'Churches, for the most part, have failed to address the nagging anxieties and deep-seated fears of the people, focusing instead upon outdated or secondary issues and proposing tired and trite solutions.'[1]

My religious label of 'Protestant' was an accident of birth. It was not of my choosing, and I have learned to value some of the richness of my inheritance, but to question some of the extremes. There has also been a journey whereby I have found the loveliness of Jesus in people who inherited a Catholic label and have a faith journey in a different church context. I have found it helpful to read of how other people who were born into this divided society have explained the religious label we all inherit. Mary McAleese describes it beautifully: 'No sooner had I taken my first breath than, as a result of tradition, circumstance of birth and parentage, I was assigned to one side of the Boyne battlefield: the Catholic Jacobite side.'[2] As a Protestant, I found myself on the other side of this battlefield.

I was baptised and confirmed in the Church of Ireland and years later was ordained deacon and priest. Then, decades later, I was ordained a bishop. In terms of denominations, my own family history includes Presbyterian, Non-Subscribing Presbyterian and, according to an Abernethy I once met in Cork, some Catholic genes as well, although I have never been able to prove or disprove that claim. All of us have different stories to tell. Growing up on a small island, we probably all have a chequered family history in terms of religious affiliation.

During my childhood I went to the celebrations on the Twelfth of July. The Orange Order paraded to celebrate King William's victory at the Battle of the Boyne in 1690. As a teenager I marched twice on this day, playing a cornet in a band. We were a silver band playing marches and were often applauded as we marched. Having observed these parades for years, from a distance, and in the cause of mutual understanding, I find the words of Mary McAleese challenging: 'They were accompanied by sashaying tartaned flute bands and, usually, a rabble wont to sing blood-curdling folk songs. It was not a Catholic-friendly event.'[3]

The history of our conflict is complicated. It was as a student at Queen's University, Belfast, that I studied the history of our divided society and discovered that there are many different ways of viewing our complicated past. There are many narratives and it is important to hear them all. Suffice to say, at this point I was someone who was born a Protestant and thereby was expected to be a unionist. This inherited label is one I have struggled with, for reasons that are important to me. There is the suggestion that the Troubles in Northern Ireland were a battle between people of different churches or faith communities. But, in fact, the divisions in our community are about identity and cultural differences that are rooted deep within our history. The struggle over land and flags has nothing to do with the Jesus that I have tried to follow. Yet so often we make it so much harder to discover this Jesus.

I was six years old when our family life changed forever. It was a cloudy day and my 'poppy' (maternal grandfather) collected me from school and brought me home. But 'home' was not the house I had left that morning, but the house where my poppy and granny lived. After I left for school the bailiffs had arrived and informed my mum that they were seizing our home to pay my father's gambling debts. My mother was evicted with our clothes and a few of our belongings. My father had gambled away our home and his family legacy.

We were given every possible support from my grandparents and my mother's siblings and their families, but as children our lives would never be the same again, and for me the scars are still present. It was years later that I realised the truth of the following: 'Pain has an amazing ability to open us to new truth and to get us moving.'[4] My grandparents and my mother did not discuss what had happened and my father was never mentioned. My brother and I did meet him one time that I remember, but I am told he left us in the pub while he went to the bookie's next door. At six years of age I did not have the ability to understand what had happened. The view of those who cared for me was that their responsibility was to protect, love and care for me. They did this wonderfully, but in not talking about what had happened I was left with unanswered questions and self-doubt. I was haunted by fear. As a child I would sit at the top of the stairs at night, frightened of the dark, unwilling to go to sleep in case my mother disappeared as well.

The next few years are sketchy in my memory, but we moved a few times after that day. Initially we stayed with my maternal grandparents, who were a special pair – they eventually celebrated sixty years of marriage. My poppy was a man of few words but amazing wisdom. He was such an important influence on me. His quiet faith was lived out and not trumpeted. In the middle of the chaos caused by my father, he was a role model for me, and a parable of love and grace. My granny's cooking and baking were a blessing. Her strength of character, kind acts and steadying presence helped us all in those extraordinary days. Like my poppy, she had a quiet faith and they were both found in their local parish church every Sunday. They also shared a passion for indoor bowls and were founding members of the parish bowling club.

As a young child I was given love and support, but the details are vague, as events just happened without explanation or information. However, there are moments that are very clear to me. There was a brief stay in our own rented home not far from our primary school, Harding Memorial. I do remember we had Catholic neighbours and we played very happily together, although I realise now that not all the children in our road mixed with them. The silence and secrecy of sectarianism were very present even then. This was in the mid-1960s before the period known as 'The Troubles' had commenced.

The next move was to a large three-storey terraced house on the Woodstock Road, opposite Willowfield police station. I believe my grandparents bought this home and they moved in with us. This was a great help to my mother who, as a lady in her late forties, had to find employment and childcare. She had married later in life and I was born when she was forty-two. This was a home that was to shape the rest of my childhood and teenage years. It had two reception rooms and a kitchen. There was a back garden and a covered yard for our bikes and the clothes wringer for drying the laundry. The first flight of stairs led to the bathroom and toilet. Another short flight of stairs led to two bedrooms, the larger one occupied by my grandparents and the smaller one at the back of the house by my mother. Then it was up another two flights of stairs to the two attic rooms. The larger room at the front of the house was the one my brother and I shared as a bedroom. The small room at the back of the house was a storeroom housing, among other items, my granny's Singer sewing machine. After a few years my grandparents left us in this home and moved to rented accommodation. I was not told, but I assume they gave the house to my mother. Their kindness and selflessness were incredible gifts in the middle of such trauma.

The most important aspect of this house for my journey of life and faith was the fact that it was very close to the parish church of Willowfield. It was also at the heart of Protestant East Belfast. When we moved there we had Catholic neighbours, but as the Troubles erupted many left or were burnt out of their homes.

My mother sought to give her children the best she could. She refused to get a divorce and I understand she paid off some of my father's debts. Her resilience, faith and generosity (with very little) were very special. However, she was emotionally scarred by what my father had done. She found it difficult to express her emotions and was uncomfortable being tactile; there were not many hugs or cuddles. This meant that my childhood was a lonely place and I was an insecure child. My childhood was not unhappy, but the trauma of my father's gambling left much pain and unspoken grief.

My mother was a woman who showed remarkable tolerance and openness to those of other church backgrounds. She taught us to value all and not to question others because of their religious affiliation. She herself had Catholic friends who were supportive of her and whom she valued greatly. The job that she managed to obtain, as a bookkeeper, was with a Jewish family, who treated her very well.

It was fun to go shopping with my mother, usually on a Friday evening after she came home from work. We would walk round the local Co-op and I would carry the basket (there were no trolleys then). When we got to the checkout she would tell the person at the till (I think always a woman) how much the bill was before the lady had checked all the items. She was always correct: her ability with numbers was outstanding. In her circumstances every penny was precious.

On reflection, I can see how my mother struggled with some members of our local parish church. Her faith in God never wavered; she would often tell us that when she needed help, particularly with finances, something would happen to help her. That faith in God sustained her through some very dark and lonely days. However, the church found it more difficult. My wider family were very involved in the local parish and had been for many years. The rector was kind to my mother and especially to me: I almost became the fourth son of the rectory. As I observed the life of ministry, I believe there was the beginning of a call. However, for the more zealous in the parish my mother was an embarrassment. They did not know what to do or what to say. These well-meaning Christians were so busy being self-righteous they forgot that the basis of our faith is grace. Free, undeserved and overwhelming grace. And grace means there is nothing I can do to make God love me more, and nothing I can do to make God love me less.'[5]

My early experience of church was filtered through the awareness that my mother found it a difficult place. In the context of a Protestant evangelical culture it was sometimes hard to find grace. There were many unwritten rules and obligations to be met. These included Sunday observance and no dancing, smoking, or alcohol, to name a few. My impression as a child was that there was not a lot of fun in following Jesus. Sunday worship was for adults and not welcoming or inclusive of children. I went because I was taken, and despite some super Sunday school teachers, it is surprising that I eventually found myself ordained.

One of the gifts I received in Sunday school was from a teacher who encouraged me to ask questions. I have always been someone who doubts, probes and does not want black-and-white answers. In fact, I believe that the questions are more important than the answers. The local parish was known as being low-church evangelical in the context of the Church of Ireland. As I look back, I am forever grateful that in that context I learned so much about the Bible and indeed learned scripture passages verbatim. These gifts have been a great blessing in my own journey of faith. However, it is also true that in Northern Ireland the Bible has been used as a weapon to hurt others, rather than point us to 'the word made flesh' (Jn 1:14).

In the 1960s most people went to church; it was expected and the normal practice. I grew up in an area where there was a Catholic congregation nearby, but there were no joint services or expressions of Christian unity. The divide was clear and from my experience there was no attempt to change that. In our home there was an acceptance of others, but in the local culture there was an underlying suspicion of those who worshipped in a different place. In fact, it is fair to say that there was an understanding that they were different faiths, not different branches of the Christian Church. From a Protestant perspective, there was the sense that Catholics could not be Christian. The regulations of the Catholic Church did not recognise me as a communicant member of Christ's Church. Vatican II was asking some great questions and making radical changes around the mid-1960s, but this good news had not filtered down to the streets of Belfast. The Troubles were just beginning to impact our lives in Northern Ireland.

During these years I was attending Harding Memorial School on the Cregagh Road. It was walking distance from our home and I loved being a pupil there. I enjoyed the work, the sport, the friends and most of the teachers. In fact, during my school years I was convinced that I was going to be a teacher. One of the reasons I particularly enjoyed Harding Memorial is that I played on the school football team – and we had a good team. We played against other Belfast primary schools, but all of them were Protestant ones.

As well as playing football at school, I also played for the Junior Boys' Brigade team. We played on a Saturday morning and it was a great start to the weekend. In our family, football was an obsession. We watched *Match of the Day* with our poppy and we just loved the game. At every opportunity we played football, and the local boy who blazed the trail was George Best. He was at the high point of his career when I was still at primary school. At a difficult time in the life of Northern Ireland, football was a great way for boys like me to do normal things. I believe there were many young boys like myself who had the dream of playing football as a profession. The dream for me was to play for Manchester United at Old Trafford. Obviously this dream never became a reality, but I have been to Old Trafford to watch many a game since!

The event that decided my future, in the world of education at least, was the Saturday that the envelopes dropped through our letterbox to inform me of the result of the dreaded 'eleven-plus'.

This meant that I had passed, as one envelope contained my result and the other was from the grammar school offering me a place. My school of choice was Grosvenor Grammar School. My brother was already at the school, just finishing his third year. I was delighted and excited about this new chapter. However, it has become apparent to me since that this was the moment I was given a future, as this strange exam opened up opportunities that many others did not get. The assumption was very clear that if you did not pass the eleven-plus you were a 'failure'. This was a dreadful moment for many young people. Some recovered, but others lived with the stigma of failure for the rest of their lives. Academic selection at the age of eleven (I had just turned eleven in the April of that school year) was unfair and unjust. I was one of the lucky ones who was given possibilities denied to others.

I started at Grosvenor in 1968, a year that is embedded in the history of Northern Ireland. It is often recognised as the year the Troubles began. A civil rights march in Derry was banned but it went ahead in defiance. The RUC tried to break up the march using water cannons and the events were captured on film and broadcast around the world. The seeds of discontent had been around for years. Catholics rightly complained of unfair treatment by the largely Protestant establishment, especially when it came to gerrymandering, jobs and housing. On reflection, I have found it sad that the establishment denied the unfair treatment of Catholics. Indeed there has often been a refusal by some Protestants to admit how Catholics were treated as second-class citizens.

Those seeds of discontent were planted years before and I find the following article in the *Guardian* insightful:

Partition. Six counties in the north of the island opt to stay in the United Kingdom when the rest of Ireland becomes independent and later a republic. Many of the inhabitants are descended from Protestant settlers brought in by James I in the 17th century, although there is still a Catholic minority, just as there continues to be a significant Protestant minority in the Republic.[6]

As I draw this chapter to a close, I want to reflect on my faith experiences during the early years of my life. My own journey of faith in these years was through my mother and grandparents. I lived through their faith as I witnessed it carrying them through what must have been excruciatingly painful days. My mother was profoundly hurt and betrayed by my father and yet she did all she could to give my brother and me every chance to live our lives to the full. She often did without so that she could provide for us. She focused on what she had rather than what she did not have. She exhibited a quiet and resolute faith in God, even though she found it hard to trust others and almost impossible to express her emotions. The support she received from her parents, siblings and wider family circle was wonderful and that support was always there for her two boys.

However, it was her faith in God that was evident to me. This was despite the difficulties she experienced with some fellow disciples. Her reputation was in tatters. To be separated or divorced was something that damaged religious credibility, and it was not possible then to be a member of the Mothers' Union if you were separated or divorced. Thankfully this has since changed, but my mum at a critical moment in her life did not receive compassion or acceptance from some of Christ's people. As a single parent and someone from a failed marriage, my mother undoubtedly felt excluded. She did everything in her power to honour her vows, but she was still deemed unworthy. I am reminded of the following reflection on the gospel narrative:

Jesus' response to suffering people and to 'nobodies' provides a glimpse into the heart of God. God is not the unmoved Absolute, but rather the Loving One who draws near. God looks on me in all my weakness, I believe, as Jesus looked on the widow standing by her son's bier, and on Simon the Leper, and on another Simon, Peter, who cursed him yet even so was commissioned to found and lead his church community, a community that need always find a place for rejects.[7]

I realised at a very young age that grace is something the Church found difficult to dispense. This was to challenge, inspire and motivate me as my journey with Jesus developed.

Within the last few years I have had the wonderful experience of becoming a grandfather. Liz and I are enjoying the delight there is in being grandparents. Patrick, Ruairi and Harris are such joy givers and they have enriched our lives. I am called 'Poppy' in honour of one man who profoundly shaped my life and faith.

One of my reactions to the trauma of what happened with my parents was to steal. I usually stole from my granny's purse – I hasten to add it was very small amounts. One particular day before I went to school I stole a coin from her 'kitty' purse, which was used to pay messages and bills. It was kept in the bottom drawer of the sideboard in the living room. When I came home from school my poppy came to my bedroom and told me he knew I had taken money from Granny's purse. He then told me to put it back and that he was going out to the corner shop to allow me to do so. Thankfully, I had not spent the money and I was able to put it back in the purse. I dreaded the evening meal, although I am not sure whether I was more anxious about my mother or my granny. During the meal nothing was said, but later that evening Poppy told me he would never tell anyone what had happened and he hoped I wouldn't do it again. He also added that he loved me and forgave me. Until the day he died, which was more than ten years later, he never mentioned it again. Years later I asked my mum about the incident; she knew nothing about it.

From my perspective, this was a modern-day parable. The irony, in my mind, is particularly poignant. I had sinned, but was forgiven and accepted. My mother, who had married a gambler, an addict, did not receive the same compassion and grace. Jesus had the uncanny ability to look at everyone with grace-healed eyes, seeing not only the beauty of who they were but also the sacred potential of what they could become. We his followers have the same challenge: "So from now on we regard no one from a worldly point of view," Paul told the Corinthians.[8]

This ability to see people through grace-filled eyes was something I discovered at a very formative time in my development, not just by words but by the actions of a man of quiet, gentle and wise faith. For that, I am forever grateful and more than proud to be called 'Poppy'.

JIM > The Island

I grew up on an island. I write not only in a literal sense of the island of Ireland, but in a figurative sense in that I grew up in the heart of West Belfast. How was that an island? you might ask. Well, it was an island of perceived Catholic nationalism/republicanism, cut off from any contact with people from outside those traditions. I use the past tense, saying that it 'was' such an island, because, thankfully, nowadays the place where I grew up and still live is not so cut off from other traditions. But more of that later.

It was to that island that I came to live in 1973, when I was just under two years of age. When my parents married and then went on to have me in 1971, their first child of four, we lived for a short time in Ligoneil on the outskirts of North Belfast. Sadly, it was the beginning of what would become a most brutal phase of the Troubles (I am wary of that euphemism as it seems to severely underplay the horror of the conflict that has torn our people apart) that befell our city and our land. Given the level of violence and death close to their new home in Ligoneil – and worried for me, this new, vulnerable life in their care – my parents sought to 'get out of Dodge', so to speak.

As luck would have it, and in a tale that is very much of its time, my parents found a new home on the Glen Road in West Belfast. Looking back now, I can see that they (and I) were part of what was, at that time, one of the biggest enforced movements of people in Europe, as people from all over Belfast moved from areas where there was violence or were forced to move, because of their religious or political affiliations, into communities marked almost exclusively as single-identity – Protestant or Catholic alone. Being only eighteen months old at the time, I had no idea that I was part of this moment in history, of course. I also had no idea at the time of the mechanism that my parents employed to get their new home. However, it was a story retold many times when I was young. It goes that my mother's cousin, who would come to be known to me as my beloved Aunt Roseleen, phoned her while they were in Ligoneil to say that her neighbour had died some weeks previous and that the house was still lying unoccupied. My father decided that desperate times called for desperate measures and so he crossed the city to the Glen Road, scrambled over the back wall of the house next to my Aunt Roseleen, climbed the drain pipe, forced the window of the back bedroom, and claimed squatter's rights – and, by God, he got his family a new home, far away from the horror of North Belfast, on the island of West Belfast!

And that was where I grew up. It was a good place for a child in many ways. Although now firmly inside the city limits and part of a very urban setting, the Glen Road of the 1970s was semi-rural. I smile to myself now as I walk the road and see apartment buildings where once were fields with horses and apple trees and ruins of old country houses. I remember spending much of my time outdoors, playing football, hurling, handball and all manner of 'chasies' games involving hiding from and/or chasing groups of other boys and girls until all were caught or freed. The population in that part of West Belfast had grown in those years, with the movement of people I described above, and as a result I had a ready-made cohort of children in and around my age to run and play with. Happy days indeed.

And yet, during these happy days, the conflict was never far away. One example of many that I recall happened around the turn of the decade between 1979 and 1980. I was outside playing rounders, a game that seems to have been a hybrid between cricket and baseball, but played with a tennis racquet. One of my friends began the interchange.

'Hey, look at yer man with the false face on!' The bowler in our game of rounders dropped the ball at his feet and pointed to the bottom of the street.

'Stop spoofing and bowl the ball. Just 'cos youse are getting bate.' The batsman was cynical about this pause, poised as he and the rest of our team were to clinch victory in this game that had been going on for most of the afternoon.

'Serious, youse-uns, look. Jesus, there's another one with a false face.'

Given that he did indeed now sound serious, if not a little frightened, we looked. There at the bottom of our street, some fifty yards away, stood two grown men, dressed normally except for two things: they were both wearing gloves on what was a warm summer afternoon and, just as our bowler had told us, they both wore the *Halloween-* (the horror film) style masks that we called 'false faces'.

Now, from a twenty-first-century adult perspective, this image could evoke a horror movie scene, but given that in 1980 none of us had ever seen a horror movie, it evoked an initial reaction of curiosity and confusion.

'Look at the hack of them!'

'They mustn't be right in the head.'

They stood on separate sides of the street, one at each corner, and through the eye slits of their false faces they were scanning up and down the road. They were clearly on edge.

As we stood and stared at them, an old woman walked up to us. She stopped and took in the sight of the false-faced men. She sighed and turned to us.

'Alright boys, listen to me. Off you go. Go home now. Are you listening to me? I'm serious. Skedaddle on home!'

There was something in her voice that told us not to argue. We parted company and went to our houses dotted here and there up the street. When I got to my door, I rushed in eager to tell of the strange sight at the bottom of the street. I went to the kitchen where my mother was peeling potatoes for the dinner.

'Mummy, wait till you hear!'

'What, son?'

'There's two men at the bottom of the street wearing false faces.'

My mum faltered ever so slightly peeling the potatoes. I noticed a slight pause before she spoke.

'Now, son. Come on. You must have made a mistake.'

'No, mummy. Some old woman saw them too and told us to go home.'

'Okay, okay. Never mind. Go on into the living room and put on the TV. *Starsky & Hutch* will be starting soon. I'll have your dinner ready in ten minutes.'

She was unsettled, I could tell, but I couldn't understand why. Why was the news about the two men at the bottom of the street such a big deal? I went into the living room and turned the TV on. A few seconds later I heard my mother leave the kitchen and go up the stairs. We lived in a small two-up, two-down house and sound carried easily. Upstairs I heard my mother and father speaking for a short while before two sets of feet were heard coming back down. There was urgency in their step. My parents went to the door. I followed behind. They went to the front gate and looked down the street. Some of my friends must have done the same as I had because there were now six or seven sets of parents out at front doors or front gates looking down the street. The two men were still there and they had been joined by some others who were standing at the front of one of the houses near the bottom of the street. My father left the garden to speak to one of the neighbours. After a short, intense-looking conversation he came back.

'It's okay. 'Mon inside here.' He beckoned my mother and me inside. Once we closed the door, he said, 'Everything will be okay now. Just forget about that. It's nothing.'

Whatever it was, I knew it wasn't 'nothing'. But he seemed pretty serious about forgetting about it so I didn't ask him any more. However, I saw that he joined my mother in the kitchen and I heard the muffled sound of them talking – no doubt about nothing!

And so that day came and went. I watched *Starsky & Hutch* and went to bed as normal.

Next morning, I asked if I could go out to call for my friends and my mother said I could. We congregated once more at the bottom of the street. All looked normal, save for one thing. A van that was normally parked there was gone. In fact, it had been parked at the house where I had seen the men standing the night before. When we all gathered, the story unfolded between us, with everyone pitching in what he had heard.

'I heard it was the cops.'

'Don't be so stupid. Why would the cops wear false faces?'

'I'm just saying what I heard.'

'Well, don't. It wasn't the cops. It was the Ra.' (For any readers not of these parts, 'the Ra' was another name for the IRA.)

'I heard that too. They came for the van.'

'Did they get it?'

'Are you serious? Look around. Do you see it? Of course they got it.'

'Well, you're hardly going to say no, are you?'

'Not to the false faces. I heard they had guns too.'

'Me too.'

Commandeering and hijacking of vehicles was very common the whole way through the Troubles. Often the stolen vehicles were used to ferry guns or people about. Sometimes they were used for attacks.

'This is boring. Just talking. Who wants to finish that game of rounders?'

Unanimous shouts of 'aye' and 'dead on' signalled that the debrief was over. And so the whole affair was over for us, filed away in some dark part of our memories and overtaken by the next, inevitable incident to befall us and our street.

The conflict was never far away from us. And we only had each other, friends and families coming from one perspective, one experience, to reflect on the meaning of such events. We were surrounded by other Catholic/nationalist/republican areas. Given the violent times of my childhood and my youth, travelling outside of the local area was often a risky business, and save for a foray into the city centre (with plenty of others from the local area) on a Saturday afternoon when I had reached my mid to late teens, we didn't go far. Our area was much more like a village than part of a city. It had schools, churches, shops, a leisure centre and eventually its own cinema. We stayed put. Consequently, I didn't meet anyone from the Protestant community the whole way through my youth and into early adulthood. I have a friend who remarks that Catholics and Protestants in these situations lived 'parallel lives'. It's only now, in my adulthood and with the relative freedom we have to travel around our city, that I realise how dysfunctional my childhood was, and how impoverished I was for not meeting people from different religious and political backgrounds. Staying cocooned within the confines of 'ourselves alone' allows sectarianism and myth-making to breed like bacteria in a petri dish. It provides for fear and division to feel normal and necessary. And it deprives us of the opportunity to get used to meeting and talking with each other.

Looking back, I am so glad to have had the parents I did, especially given those times and the nature of our cocooned lives. I could easily have grown up as bitter or closed-minded. I must admit, of course, that I carry within me the sectarianism of my times. Never having met a Protestant allowed for all sorts of fears, worries and prejudices to cling to me in those days. However, thanks to my parents, I had some narratives to challenge that sectarianism.

Each had their own way of expressing themselves and their world view and both of these world views were informed by their faith and their image of God. My father held two mantras that he gave to me. In order of importance to him: number one – your family comes before everyone else; number two – if you live right, it will all come right in the end. What a wonderful, simple spirituality! Right living to my father was saying your prayers, working hard and treating people (particularly your family) well.

My mother expressed her world view differently. She came to it from a much more overtly religious perspective. She told me that 'there is good and bad in everyone' and that we were not to judge any group of people on the basis of how some of them behaved. In other words, I grew up knowing that she wanted me to know that Protestants were good people too. She told me stories of how she would shop on the Shankill Road as a child, walking from her home on the lower Falls Road, across Northumberland Street, enjoying the many shops right up and down the length of the Shankill. She spoke of the times before my birth when there was no violence and, while she knew that things were not right in Northern Ireland and that change had been needed, she believed in the Jesus she heard about in church, who preached non-violence and urged us to 'turn the other cheek'. And this was the Jesus she gave to me. This was the Jesus she brought me to Mass each week to encounter.

One of my favourite memories of childhood is sitting, cuddled into my mother, on a pew of our local church, St Teresa of Avila on the Glen Road, at Mass on a weekday evening. It must have been winter, because I remember that it was dark and cold outside the church. However, I was warm there, basking in the love of my mother and the lights of the candles on the altar. My mother was my evangelist – she was the one who brought me to Christ in the Church and in the Mass. She held an image of a God so loving, and she witnessed to that by being so loving herself, that I fell in love with God through her.

Consequently, I decided to get involved in the life of the Church as a child by becoming an altar boy, serving the altar during Mass at the weekend and, sometimes, during the week. I have so many good memories of being an altar boy. It gave me an insight into the Church as real community. I got to serve with other children, most of whom became firm friends. It also gave me an opportunity to get to know God through prayer and worship from an early age. I was fascinated by the ritual elements of the Catholic faith, and being an altar boy allowed me to participate directly in those rituals.

I was so taken by all of this that for a long time during my childhood and teenage years I believed that I was called to be a priest. I had some very intense conversations with priests along the way. They advised and guided me. I prayed a lot about it but, as I entered my late teenage years, I concluded that the priesthood was not for me after all. You see, I felt a deep desire to be a husband and father. Even at the tender age of sixteen, I knew that this was God's calling in my life. And, as we know, marriage and ordination to the priesthood in the Catholic tradition do not go well together! I often wonder what turns life would have taken had I been born into an Anglican or Presbyterian or Methodist family. Might ordination have been part of my life journey? Who knows. What I do know is that I was born into a good and faithful family and that God has a plan for everyone. Mine was to take a very strange route.

REFLECTION

Alan and Jim have highlighted the following issues in this chapter:
1. Religious labels
2. Faith and conflict
3. Family influence

Reflect
In what ways do you see these issues in your own life experience?

Challenge
Having read these reflections, in what way do you hear God challenging you to discover Jesus in the other?

Pray
Matthew 12:46-50
John 4:1-27

NOTES

1. Eddie Gibbs and Ian Coffey, *Church Next: Quantum Changes in Christian Ministry*, Illinois: InterVarsity Press, 2001, p. 20.
2. Mary McAleese, *Here's the Story: A Memoir*, Dublin: Penguin Ireland, 2020, p. 19.
3. *Ibid.*, p. 20.
4. Peter Scazzero, *Emotionally Healthy Spirituality*, Grand Rapids, MI: Zondervan, 2017, p. 19.
5. Philip Yancey, *What's So Amazing About Grace?*, Grand Rapids, MI: Zondervan, 1997, p. 71.
6. Sean Clarke, James Sturcke and Jenny Percival, 'Timeline: Northern Ireland', *Guardian* (London), 10 March 2009.
7. Philip Yancey, *The Jesus I Never Knew*, Grand Rapids, MI: Zondervan, 1995, p. 161.
8. Richard Rohr, *Breathing Under Water: Spirituality and the Twelve Steps*, London: SPCK Publishing, new edition, 2018, p. 48.

CHAPTER TWO
Education, Church and Growing Up

ALAN > An Odd Normality

Everything was new. The school uniform, including short trousers and cap. The school buildings and a timetable that meant we had to move classrooms for each subject. Different teachers for all subjects – and so many subjects. The first few days were mesmerising. Although there were a few children from my primary school, there were many I had not met before, and I had lost my position as one of the senior pupils.

Then there was the shock of having to play rugby, made worse by the fact that my older brother was a very good rugby player. My position was already chosen because of my brother: scrum-half. I was unable to get excited about this game. Perhaps it was the strange shape of the ball or maybe it was the hard physical contact. Playing scrum-half placed me at the heart of the action, and the opposing forwards were always much bigger than me. I did manage to play some games, but I did not make the grade as a rugby player and that did not disappoint me. My first love in sport was and has remained football.

I was also introduced to the possibility of playing a musical instrument. The trombone was the one I wanted, but I had to settle for a trumpet. Throughout my school years I had the joy of playing in the school orchestra and school band, made great fun mainly thanks to our enthusiastic music teacher. This led me to playing in a local band, Bloomfield Silver Band, which introduced me to playing the cornet while marching. We even played Beethoven's Fifth Symphony as a competition piece. I found myself marching on the first of July through East Belfast on what was known as the 'Mini-Twelfth'. However, the big event was the Twelfth of July, a major celebration of the Protestant victory at the Battle of the Boyne in 1690 – a day of marching, eating, speeches, crowds cheering and, in some cases, imbibing too much alcohol. I took part in this day twice as a teenager and was amazed at how our silver band was applauded as we marched. We played marching tunes and not the sectarian tunes that were to become the norm.

Our family finances were always tight and my brother and I were always keen to help. I followed in his footsteps and became a paper boy. A local newsagent, Cowan's, at the corner of Titania Street and the Cregagh Road, employed young boys, although later there were also paper girls. I was ten when I started this job. Every morning before school I would deliver the morning paper to customers who had ordered their newspaper of choice and wanted it delivered. There would be about thirty to forty papers to deliver. This covered an area within a certain radius from the shop and there were four different runs (areas for delivery). After school there was the early edition of the *Belfast Telegraph*, known as the 'Fourth'. Then after 5.30 there was the later edition of the same newspaper, called the 'Sixth'. The number of newspapers varied depending on how far the run was from the shop. I was doing this until I was seventeen. The largest run, with nearly one hundred copies of the Sixth, was the one closest to the shop. This delivery was completed on my bicycle with a special bag for carrying the papers.

On the run furthest from the shop I would come into contact with pupils from different schools on their way home. Occasionally

I would be aware that pupils from a local Catholic school knew I was different and went to a different school. It was intimidating, but it was only name-calling and nothing physical. Which side you belonged to in this divided society was always obvious by what school you attended. Even to this day I will not ask anyone from Northern Ireland I meet when travelling, 'What school did you go to?' For someone from Northern Ireland this is a loaded question that can be uncomfortable, a reminder of the deep divisions of home.

One of the joys of delivering papers was Christmas. Most customers would give a Christmas tip and it was always interesting how it took me much longer delivering the papers the few weeks before Christmas. This was to allow time for the customer to get to the door and ensure that I got that tip I was hoping for! Over the years I did very well out of Christmas tips. It made it all the more exciting to go shopping after Christmas.

The year I started Grosvenor has been recognised by many as the start of what came to be known as the Troubles. These were the years when I was a teenager and a young adult. It is in retrospect that I am able to see how the tapestry of happenings during these formative years shaped my future life and ministry.

It is very obvious that my schooling was part of the division in our society. I enjoyed school in general; it gave me an academic foundation that helped me discover my vocation and the necessary qualifications to facilitate that calling. However, the fact was that, through the early tragic days of the Troubles, I was not able to cross that divide, and my schooling actually accentuated the division. It makes me sad that this educational divide persists today. We must find ways of doing this differently or we simply perpetuate the misunderstanding and prejudice:

Only mutual apology, healing, and forgiveness offer a sustainable future for humanity. Otherwise we are controlled by the past, individually and corporately. We all need to apologise, and we all need to forgive, or this human project will surely self-destruct. No wonder that almost two-thirds of Jesus' teaching is directly or indirectly about forgiveness. Otherwise, history winds down into the taking of sides, deep bitterness, and remembered hurts, plus the violence that inevitably follows.

My journey of faith during these years was lukewarm, although during the summer holidays it became much more animated. This was due to my attendance at certain summer camps. With our family's finances, summer holidays were not possible, but we did have great fun joining our cousins and my maternal grandparents at different holiday homes for many years. During my teenage years, even though my faith was half-hearted, I was involved in many church activities, and my home parish of Willowfield was a strong supporter of the Bible Church Missionary Society. This mission agency held summer camps for teenagers that I attended in Sutton, north Dublin, and later in Greystones, Co. Wicklow. These camps were a formative influence on me. Although I drifted through my teenage years, struggling with myself, my context and the relevance of faith, my time at these camps was an anchor that somehow kept me in touch with Jesus.

The camps, situated in church halls, were fun-filled and activity-based, with a gentle emphasis on personal faith. There were daily chores, daily Bible studies, short sermons, day trips and good food. Each year I would be aware of the call of Jesus to be a disciple and it was easy while I was at camp. However, during the years between these camps I would return to a lukewarm faith. It was some of the leaders who shaped me and attracted me to Jesus. Their vibrant faith, sense of fun and willingness to let me ask questions were gently drawing me to my future and a more focused journey of faith. As a student, I was ultimately to become a leader of these camps myself.

The daily life of growing up in a divided city and land was an odd normality. There were army patrols, stop-and-search road blocks, bomb scares and the huge security gates in Belfast city centre. My mum had to return to work after my dad disappeared and she was employed by Solomon and Peres as a bookkeeper. They owned a local recording company and The Gramophone Shop on Donegall Square North. The owner of this company was Jewish and it was fascinating learning about some of their religious practices. This was a refreshing experience, and my mum was a helpful teacher of mutual acceptance and respect.

As a result of my mum's work, I managed to get a summer job in The Gramophone Shop while still at school. It later involved Christmas and Easter holidays. In due course, I was also employed on Saturday mornings, leaving me free to play football on Saturday afternoons. The staff were great fun and came from very different faith backgrounds, which was a positive experience in the midst of an increasingly polarised religious community. It is one of the great lessons of my teenage years that people are not defined by religious labels, but are individuals with a personal story. So often we do not listen to those stories because we judge people by their religious label or, in Northern Ireland, by the school they attended or the faith community they belong to. Working in the city centre also brought me face to face with security barriers and being searched as you entered every shop. Indeed there were days when I had to stand at the door of the shop and examine people's bags as they entered. That was the norm growing up in Northern Ireland in those strange days.

Living on the Woodstock Road also brought me into contact with the frightening world of paramilitaries, intimidation and riots. Our home was directly opposite the local RUC station, Willowfield police station. To the right of our home was my local church, Willowfield Church. To the left of our home was St Anthony's Parish Catholic Church. Behind it was a school, a convent and the parochial house.

There was growing tension in Northern Ireland during these days, the early 1970s. Riots and attacks on the police became common in loyalist and republican areas. People were burnt out of their homes if they had a different religious label to those who lived in that locality. Many of our Catholic neighbours left their homes during this period, fearing for their property and lives. They were not welcome in an area becoming increasingly loyalist and Protestant. There were petrol bomb attacks and an uneasy atmosphere on the streets. It was not safe to walk in certain parts of the city and life became focused on the local. I found my safe place in the parish church, with its own football team and tennis club and courts.

***

It was a moment that shaped me, and will disturb me for the rest of my life. The events of that evening made me ask life-changing questions about the faith culture that I had inherited.

It was a period of particular tension in East Belfast. There was general unease that another riot could happen at any time. I was getting ready for bed, and at the same time observing an ever-growing crowd gathering a few hundred yards from our home. They had been encouraged by the language of hate and division. I was terrified, as I could almost taste the rage in the air. I was hiding behind the curtains in our upstairs front bedroom, watching the scene unfold. The mob attacked the police station opposite our house, throwing bricks, bottles and anything they could get their hands on. I was transfixed.

Two shots rang out, fired into the air from the police station. The rioters quickly moved away from the police station towards to St Anthony's Catholic Church in the next block. They broke the doors down and proceeded to desecrate it. They destroyed statues and confession boxes, leaving the main road littered with debris.

I felt huge relief when I saw army patrols arrive at the scene. The rioters slowly dispersed, leaving carnage in their wake. It was the following morning when I saw the full horror of what had happened. I witnessed the distress of a local church community and, at the same time, the presence of other church communities who had come to help.

This was a momentous occasion in my struggle with faith, Jesus and the so-called religious war taking place before my eyes. The constant news of sectarian killings, of politicians squabbling and point-scoring, was the daily backcloth of my teenage years. Alongside this, while I wrestled with this Jesus who so attracted me, many of his representatives appeared to talk a language of mistrust, suspicion and, at times, hate.

I found myself grappling with some of the unwritten codes of behaviour in our community. There was a mentality of 'them and us' in this society deeply divided along religious and political lines. The polarisation was often hidden behind key phrases such as 'They are nice people but …' or 'I am not sure you can trust them because …' This division, mistrust and pain are still very real in our local communities.

From the night I witnessed a riot outside my home, I knew that if faith was to mean anything, it must lead to reaching across the hurt and pain of this tortured land. I would not have used the word then, but reconciliation is at the heart of the message of Jesus and it needs to be at the heart of any discipleship that seeks to follow Jesus today: 'Reconciliation is an ongoing spiritual process involving forgiveness, repentance and justice that restores broken relationships and systems to reflect God's original intention for all creation to flourish.'

As I journeyed through my school years I was never top of the class, but generally average. The subjects that I eventually studied to A level were history, English and maths. I had dabbled with the idea of following my paternal grandfather as an optician, but the need for the three sciences made that impossible. A major discovery during my O level years was that I was colour-blind and hence was encouraged not to study geography any more. The maps were impossible for me, with their mixture and array of colours and contours. I had discovered the joy of reading in primary school and that enabled me to enjoy history and English. My mother and my poppy were brilliant with numbers and I must have inherited some of their genes, as maths was also a subject I enjoyed. In my final two years of school, because of a wonderful English teacher, I also discovered the delights of Shakespeare and Thomas Hardy. I can still recite some of the lines from *The Merchant of Venice* and *Hamlet*.

I was beginning to think about life after school and my thoughts were leading me in the direction of training as a teacher. There is no doubt that I had been influenced by those who taught me – teachers who inspired, encouraged and made their subjects interesting due to their own enthusiasm about the material. At this stage I was keen to teach history and physical education. During my last year at school, a stressful and fascinating year, the applications were made for third-level education. However, my life was turned upside down by my poppy's death and a series of events in the local parish church.

He was such an important figure in my life, with his unconditional love and his gentle but firm discipline. The faith that captured him at a young age was evident in his life. There was a calmness, a wisdom and an acceptance that drew you into his care. It was my dream from a young age to be like him and I have prayed throughout my life to be given the wisdom he had. The first stroke debilitated him and left him with some paralysis, but the most distressing part was that his speech was affected. He knew what he wanted to say, but to his immense frustration he couldn't articulate the words. Then there was another major stroke from which he never recovered. He died in the City Hospital. I loved this man. He was not only my poppy, but my surrogate father. His presence in my life was an amazing gift through a traumatic childhood. The death of someone I loved, someone who was on my side, left me thinking even more about my life after school.

At the same time there was a series of meetings in my parish church. I do not remember a time when I did not believe, but during this week I found myself being challenged to follow Jesus as an active disciple rather than being passive. This was a grace moment that dragged me into a very different future from what I had been planning. Within months, I was a youth club leader, a Sunday School teacher, and had preached my first sermon. It was unnerving, but very quickly the shadow of ordination loomed large, with the encouragement of friends, clergy and many who knew me in the local church. My mum was cautious but supportive. The next chapter of my life was taking shape, but first I was to become a student at Queen's University, Belfast. My chosen course of study was history and political science.

It was the love and influence of family, teachers and a church community that had brought me thus far. A church community that was flawed. A religious environment that made me question and struggle with sectarianism and self-righteousness. A family that, despite our difficult and painful experience, gave me a great deal of love and glimpses of faith in action much more powerful than words. I was called to be a disciple of Jesus in the confusion, hurt and pain of life and in the fractured community of Northern Ireland. This call grew out of a reaction to the anger and hate of the 'other' and was rooted in the love of a person called Jesus. In the words of Michael Perham, 'Being a disciple of Jesus is never about joining an exclusive sect, always about the desire to embrace the whole of humanity.'

The classroom shook silently for a second before the noise reached our ears. When it did, it was a low thud followed by a deafening rumble. We all knew what it was; we'd heard many explosions before. This time was only different in scale. It was louder and we shook more vigorously than the other times.

Primary 7 after the eleven-plus was a time filled with new things. The pressure was off now. No more preparing for the test. Both teachers and pupils could relax a bit. Mr Glover, my Primary 7 teacher in St Teresa's Primary School, was teaching us some words of French. It was 24 May 1983.

After the blast, instinctively I turned towards the window of the classroom that looked out onto the Glen Road and down towards the city centre. I could measure the proximity of the bomb by the closeness of the smoke. The smoke was very close and intensely black. Someone shouted, 'That'll be the barracks again.'

The Andersonstown police station, known locally as 'the barracks', would become one of the most bombed stations in the North by the end of the Troubles. By May 1983 it had already been the scene of many mortar, gun and bomb attacks and so it came as no surprise to us that this seemed to be where the cloud of smoke was emanating from. However, the din of the noise and the size of the smoke cloud did serve to disconcert us and freeze us in place. We probably only looked out the window for a few moments before moving but it felt like we stared into the smoke for an eternity.

Soon after the bomb, we were sent home. Home for me was closer to the barracks than the school was and so I was travelling towards and into the chaos, as opposed to further away from it. There was the customary noise of sirens and heavily armed army vehicles speeding this way and that. I don't remember much of that walk home or of my parents' reaction once I got there. I'm told that they were very relieved to see me and my siblings – all of whom were younger than me and also at the school that day. But remember, this was a decade and more into what was essentially a guerrilla war on the streets of Belfast so, while it was a big day in many ways, it was also just another chapter in the story of mayhem unfolding before my eleven-year-old eyes.

After a while in the house, I asked my mother if I could go out with my friends if I promised to stay in the street, close to home, and definitely not go any nearer to the bomb. Judging that the bomb had gone off some time before and with the time having passed it was unlikely that there would now be a follow-up gun attack, she said I could, and I left the house, picked up one of my friends in the street, and duly went as close to the bomb site as possible. We found the Glen Road blocked by a cordon and army vehicles. No way through there. So we went back up our street and through to the other streets that snake off the Glen Road. This way, we got closer to the barracks. As we did, we began to see pieces of masonry and metal strewn around the streets, blown hundreds of yards through the air and sitting incongruously in hedges and on top of sheds and car roofs. Everywhere smoke hung in the air, a stinking reminder of the stench of violence that hung over our land.

We got to one street away from the barracks and we came upon a single soldier standing in the street. This was a strange sight indeed. First, we rarely saw those guys on their own (they usually travelled in a group of four at least; I suppose today was a different day for everyone). Second, his uniform was covered in dust and his face with a mixture of black smoke and red blood, emanating from a wound at the point where his soldier's cap met his brown hairline. Even to my young eyes, I knew that this soldier was a young man himself. He was shaking. Anger? Fear? Both? He stopped us by holding his hand up. He held us with manic eyes and said, 'That was meant for you, that bomb was.'

He ushered us back to where we had come from. We left the scene and returned to our street. We didn't believe the soldier. We knew that the target of the bomb had not been us. It had been him. It had been his comrades. It had been the RUC. It had been that station that had come to represent British presence in a land where those who planted the bomb felt they had a right to kill people to rid themselves of such a presence.

It would be a few days before we got down to survey the site of the bomb. It had been a thousand-pound bomb, the biggest to have been planted to date. It caused a reported £1 million in damage. While no one was killed – almost a miracle – many people had been caught up in the blast. There were stories abounding of people being blown off their feet and through windows as well. There were lots of injuries. Houses were damaged. Some had to be destroyed. Businesses in the area suffered badly as they had to close until rebuilding took place. Many people were prescribed tranquillizers in the wake of this and other such attacks, their nerves shattered. The road was closed for six months while the barracks was rebuilt as a huge, fortified military base that would do well in the middle of Afghanistan or Syria now. Its walls were several metres thick and many metres high. It became an eyesore: a reminder of pain and suffering. The bomb might not have been aimed at us, but we all suffered nonetheless.

In 2005, the Andersonstown police station – the barracks – was once again destroyed. However, this time it wasn't a bomb. It wasn't an act of war. Ironically, peace finally brought its history to a close. It was dismantled as part of the 'normalising' after the signing of the Good Friday Agreement in 1998. Bulldozers and diggers moved in and took it all down. The ground was levelled and grass seed was scattered on the soil. Nowadays, I walk to the site of the barracks every day with my dogs. It is fenced in and once again grown over with grass and some flowers. It is used almost exclusively as a dog park, save for a few political demonstrations held on the ground each year – well, it's still West Belfast!

And that bomb will, in my mind, always be associated with the end of my primary school days and the start of my secondary school journey. I moved school during that terribly unsettled and violent year of 1983.

I didn't move too far, though. St Mary's Christian Brothers' Grammar School, my new educational home for the next seven years, was only a half-mile further up the road from St Teresa's Primary School. Moving school is not only about moving building, of course, and while it was nearby, the new school was a million miles from the experience of being the big fish in the wee pond of primary school. I was now the tiniest of wee fish in the big pond of 'big boys' school'. Being an anxious sort of person, I struggled to settle into the new school, with its huge building, new uniform and strange subjects. I looked to my mother for reassurance at that time and she helped me enormously to cope with this difficult transition.

Another source of reassurance – and this is a source of reassurance to me right to this day – was a small book of the New Testament and psalms. We were given this book at the start of our first year and I remember reading and rereading it, marvelling particularly at the Jesus story. I would sit and imagine myself back there in Galilee witnessing all the miraculous works of Jesus and hearing his words – words I did not fully understand at that time, but which seemed to be telling of a God who loved all of God's children and who gave us the reassurance of eternal life in heaven. How those sentiments were like a balm on my wound of anxiety! And how Jesus' words of peace were at odds with the society around me. Each day I would read the gospels and the psalms and then go out into a world where division and violence were the most common currencies of the day. Still, the words from the Bible were of comfort to me, and as the first couple of years of school went by I settled well into my new surroundings.

I threw myself into my studies. I played Gaelic football (soccer was banned in the school at that time – it was seen as a British sport and not appropriate for an Irish school). I got involved in the drama and music departments. School life was very vibrant indeed. Outside of school, there wasn't a lot to do. Right in the heart of West Belfast, we didn't dare stray too far from our own district for fear of meeting a violent end. And so we just hung around with our friends. We made our own fun telling jokes and stories, outdoing each other in 'slegging'. I love that Belfast word. It means to make fun of, but not in too cruel a sense. It was almost a way of life for our group of friends, and a way of bonding with each other.

We were a band of anywhere up to about ten young fellas who gathered nightly somewhere near our homes. In earlier times it had been an early-evening gathering to play football or handball against the big wall of McErlean's bakery at the top of Arizona Street. As time went on, however, our gatherings had stretched to the heady height of a nine o'clock finish and our interests had stretched out too – music and girls were now the main attractions. Between us, we had a ghetto blaster radio/cassette player (I don't know who owned that – I only know it wasn't me; we would never have had the money in our family for such an item) and some cassettes of the music we were listening to. Around that time, we decided that standing right at the bottom of our street, at the corner, gave us the two things we needed – the space to stand and listen to our music and the best possibility of seeing some girls going by. It became a routine.

We weren't a bad bunch of fellas. I don't remember us doing a lot wrong. We didn't destroy property or harass anyone. We didn't stand at the bottom of the street throwing stones at the soldiers. We were … normal kids. That said, we liked a laugh, and in particular there was one of our number who liked to fool around. He was great at telling funny stories or making fun of one of our group until we would all (including, for the most part, the one being made fun of) fall about laughing.

I remember one evening an older man stopped to ask us directions.

Old man: 'Lads, do you know where such and such a street is?'

Funny friend: 'I do.'

The rest of us: roll our eyes and wait for the punchline.

Old man: 'Thank you, son. Go ahead.'

Funny friend: 'Go down the road here and take the first right.'

Old man: 'Okay.'

Funny friend: 'Then go about fifty yards and take the next right.'

Old man: 'Next right. Right.'

Funny friend: 'Right. Right. Then go another fifty yards and take the next right.'

Old man: 'Another right. Right.'

Funny friend: 'Another right. Right. Right, go ahead another … about fifty yards and take the next right.'

Old man: silence with brows beginning to rise ever so slightly.

Funny friend: 'Then keep walking and we'll wave at you on the way past!'

Old man: realisation dawns.

The rest of us: explode with laughter.

Old man: expletives flow and then he walks off in a huff.

Yes, that friend was really funny. Most of the time he was funny. Back on that night in November 1985 when we were listening to A-ha, things were less funny. At some point during a song a police jeep, all gunmetal grey and noisy engine, drove past slowly. Our friend must have seen this and known that there would be another one coming. Sure enough, another came slowly up the street. It was a cold night and most of us wore gloves or hats or scarves,

maybe some combination of all three. Our friend had a scarf on –
a Liverpool FC scarf. For some reason (and later we were to quiz
him heavily on what the reason was), he pulled his scarf up over the
lower part of his face and gave a single-fist salute. This was the sign
of a revolutionary. In that place and at that time, it was a republican
salute.

Now, to put into context what was about to happen: he gave
this salute. He didn't do anything else. He didn't throw a stone or
a petrol bomb. He didn't carry a gun. We didn't even notice he was
doing it until it was too late to tell him to wise up. He gave this
salute and the second police jeep must have contained someone who
saw it. The jeep swerved suddenly and sped towards us. It mounted
the kerb and screeched to a halt a few feet from where we stood.
The first jeep that had passed turned in the road and similarly
came up onto the kerb at high speed and stopped beside our group,
effectively hemming us in against the wall of the building we were
standing in front of. Within a few seconds, there were five or six
policemen, each individually questioning one of us as to why we
were standing there. They searched us, took our names and made it
clear that we were not to be standing about there again.

This was the first time I had been stopped and searched by a
member of the security forces. I had turned fourteen years old the
previous month. When asked my name and address I could hardly
speak for fear. My hands and legs trembled, although I never told
my friends this at the time. For some of them, this was not their
first time being stopped. They took it in their stride, or so it seemed
to me. Maybe they were being like me, though, and not letting
anyone see how they really felt. We didn't do much sharing of deep
emotions back then. There were too many emotions to share. We
wouldn't have known where to start.

Almost as quickly as the jeeps had mounted the pavement, the
police got back in and they drove off.

One friend: 'What did you do that for?'

Funny friend: 'I dunno.'

Another friend: 'Well, don't do it again. We have to move now.'

Another friend: ''Mon up outside the Credit Union up the street. No one can see us from the road there.'

And we went up the street to what was to become our nightly gathering space – a safe haven – for years to come. I was still shaken up. Somewhere along the way, I made an excuse and went home. I burst in through the door to tell my parents about the madness that had happened and how I was searched and questioned by the police and how I hadn't done anything and how I was only a kid and how my friend was only messing about and how they could have knocked us down with the jeeps and how it all was unfair. I rambled on for a minute.

My mother and father stopped me talking and quietly told me the truth: that this was going to happen again. It was how it was in Belfast now. They told me that, although this was the first time and that it was very frightening, I would soon be used to it and it wouldn't be as scary. This was to be the new normal. They told me to always be courteous when I was stopped by a policeman or a soldier, lest I annoy them and they got rough. They then reminded me of something they had told me many times before and would again many times after – there's good in everyone and violence is wrong. They told me to remember that and it would set me in good stead. I think they were right.

They were right about being stopped again as well. It soon became a daily occurrence. For the most part it was uneventful and in the main I didn't have any feelings about it. I knew they were doing their job and that, in the mad world of Northern Ireland at that time, mad things happened. While I didn't do any of those mad things, I was there and I knew I was caught up in them.

In the midst of such uncertainty, and outside of my family, there were two things that gave me a sense of security: school and church. They both provided a routine and some predictability. Much as I resented going to school some days, as most pupils do, it gave me a community, an identity, and a place to flourish. I still remember with fondness many of the teachers I met there. One such teacher was not a teacher at all. Let me explain. When I started St Mary's, it was still staffed by Christian Brothers – men who had joined a religious order, taken vows of celibacy and obedience, and lived out their vocation as teachers in the manner of their founder, Edmund Ignatius Rice. Edmund, born in the eighteenth century, is now on his way to becoming a saint. While many Christian Brothers were no saints, and some were barely Christian in how they treated their pupils, most of the men I met were kind and talented. One in particular had retired just before I started at the school and so, when I met him, he was no longer a teacher. He operated two greenhouses on the school grounds and welcomed boys there to tend the plants and help him maintain the operation. I thank God that I was one of those boys. I spent many happy hours in his company, essentially gardening, which is an interest I have not kept up. But rather than the gardening, I was brought back there by the man and by his kind words and listening ear. He would treat us with respect and generosity, making sure we got a plant to take home to our mummies every now and then. Long before taking care of our planet was a top priority, this man knew the value of nature and encouraged us to see the world as a beautiful, God-given resource. Without ever preaching or quoting the Bible, this old man taught me about God in God's love of nature and our fellow man.

Being educated in an all-boys, all-Catholic environment, although I enjoyed it greatly, obviously had its drawbacks. I didn't learn how to talk to girls for a long time! And I still, by the time I left school at almost eighteen years of age, had never knowingly met a Protestant person. It seems so strange now, looking at my children who, having also gone to Catholic schools, have met and befriended people not only from the Protestant community but all sorts of communities. The freedoms they enjoy around movement and meeting up were just not open to me at their age. And so I was still living on an island, cut off from 'themuns' and experiencing the world from my own narrow, experiential perspective. While I don't like to admit it, I see how my views were impacted by that. I had a distrust of what 'they' might be up to. I couldn't understand the continual stops by soldiers and police; I wasn't doing anything wrong, after all. Yes, in my own way, I was sectarian. I had a sense of my own community as right and the 'other' community as wrong. Well, up to a point, that is. I struggled with my own inner sectarianism, even at that young age, although it is only now, with the benefit of hindsight and decades behind me, that I can understand it in that way. I never bought into the myths of what would have been considered by some to have been 'my own clan'. I never, ever brought myself to be able to accept violence as a legitimate course of action, whatever the provocation. In my naivety, I became a sort of hippy in my mid to late teenage years. I grew my hair, wore weird clothes and opted out of the dominant narratives of republicanism that swelled around me. I think I just knew, deep down inside, after reading that little book of the New Testament and psalms all those years before, that we were called to make peace and, as I would have thought in my childlike innocence back then, be friends. I am glad to say that I have retained some of that childlike innocence and naivety, and still think that we all should be friends!

And so I didn't go down a political or paramilitary path, like some of my friends did. I threw myself into my second source of security – the Church. I kept involved in my local parish all the way through my teens and, although I wandered far away from the Church in my twenties (the next chapter will be fun!), in my teenage years I stayed close.

As the 1980s began to come to a close and with them my school days, Northern Ireland kept burning and exploding around me. Men, women and children were dying. No end was in sight. It was in this context that I was to leave the relative safety of my home community for the first time, and go to university.

REFLECTION

Alan and Jim have highlighted the following issues in this chapter:
1. The influence of church on our lives
2. Segregated education
3. The 'odd normality' of conflict and violence influenced by religious difference

Reflect
In what ways do you see these challenges in your own life experience?

Challenge
Having read these reflections, in what way do you hear God challenging you to discover Jesus in the other?

Pray
Matthew 5:38-48
Luke 8:26-39

CHAPTER THREE

Struggles, Sectarianism and Questions

ALAN > Wrestling with Faith and Calling

It was a very exciting moment when I became a student at Queen's University, Belfast. My A level results were not as predicted and they were short of what Queen's had stipulated. However, I was accepted to study history and political science. With my personal circumstances and my mother's small income, I received a maximum grant and all my fees were paid. Those days are long gone and I realise that without this help I would not have been able to attend university.

During my years at Queen's, 1975–8, I lived at home. The journey from east to south of the city was not straightforward during those turbulent years. Mary McAleese described how it felt:

> Beyond the awful death toll, we lived with a constant, nagging, physically debilitating anxiety that accompanied the simplest things, like going to shops, getting the bus into town, coming home from school in a particular school uniform, walking home after a night out. To live in a place where your streets are not yours is to live in a nightmare.'[1]

I find it difficult to read these words, but they resonate with me as someone who lived through those years. The circumstances of Belfast during my time as a student made attending any evening activities difficult. My experience was limited to being a daytime student.

The Troubles were a cloud that hung over everyday life. It is difficult to explain as every day there was a routine to follow: lectures to attend, essays to write, seminars to prepare for and an endless reading list to be studied. However, the backcloth was one of bomb scares, tit-for-tat killings, riots, security gates in Belfast city centre, whistles blown for the last bus leaving town and bags searched entering any shop or public building.

On one occasion, I missed the last bus to the city centre. It would have been unsafe to walk home alone across the city, so I chose to stay with friends in their student flat, with a sleeping bag and a floor for the night. Reflecting on these memories reminds me of how strange student days could be in Belfast.

For most of my teenage years, my first love had been football, but during my last year at school I received a bad knee injury when playing for the local parish team. By the time it had recovered enough to let me play again, I was a student at Queen's. My hope was to join the university football team, but the problem of travelling across the city after evening training and the concern about my knee meant that it never happened. It is a regret I have lived with since because it would have brought some normality to my student experience. Instead I continued to play for the parish team, although my injury still made that troublesome.

This new world was exciting, and as a student there were many choices of clubs and societies, but living at home and the problems that brought meant I only got involved in the Christian Union. I was drawn to the Church of Ireland chaplaincy as a safe place to discuss my struggle with my calling, but I enjoyed the small groups and benefited from some of the large gatherings of the Christian Union on a Thursday. My memory is that it met at 5.00 p.m. The timing was important as it meant I could get an early-evening bus home.

The Christian Union in Queen's was a Protestant Christian group with a Bible-based evangelistic purpose. There was a strong Presbyterian and Free Church flavour. It had a specific missional focus, but there were also small groups that encouraged fellowship and mutual support. As an Anglican, a member of the Church of Ireland, I was in a tiny minority.

At the heart of my discipleship was a call to be a bridge builder and reconciler in the deep religious divisions of our community. While at Queen's I was determined to find ways of following this call. In the Christian Union this was problematic, as some of its members appeared to be sure that Roman Catholics were not true Christians. I could not identify with this. There were teachings of the Roman Catholic Church that I questioned, but I also struggled with the teaching of any denomination. There was and is no 'perfect church', as they are all full of human beings. It struck me at this time that most denominations appeared to be more interested in their own growth and survival than extending the kingdom of God. From my perspective, this was and is best achieved when we live, work and witness together. 'Let me give you a new command. Love one another. In the same way I loved you, love one another. This is how everyone will recognise that you are my disciples – when they see the love you have for each other.'[2]

In the context of Northern Ireland there is an issue that has to be highlighted at this point. From the perspective of some Protestants, Roman Catholics are not true Christians. That is a very stark comment, but it is at the heart of these reflections. Within the Christian Union, this would have been the predominant view. This is an issue that I had to resolve as my own journey and calling developed. The question that helped me on this journey was, 'Am I secure enough in my faith to listen to the stories of the "other"?' So often I witnessed Christians pulling down the drawbridge and building barricades against the 'other'. I wanted to find a way to discover Jesus in the 'other'. If my own faith was not secure enough to share stories with people who are not in 'my' group, then it was not very deep.

I was studying history and political science and very quickly I discovered a passion for politics. There was political philosophy, American politics (at the time of the Watergate scandal), European politics and the cut and thrust of debate in seminars. This was a subject that stirred something within me that has stayed with me since. Over the years, I have visited the House of Commons to watch Prime Minister's Question Time. Lady Sylvia Hermon, the Member of Parliament for North Down, my local constituency, very kindly facilitated my visits. In my first lecture at Queen's I learned the definition of politics as 'the art of the possible'. That definition has inspired me on my journey of faith.

It was in a political science lecture that I met Brendan McAllister. We were to become good friends during the next few years. He was from Newry, and our background, cultural upbringing and church affiliation were very different. However, we shared an interest in politics and a desire to share our faith stories. He was to have a profound effect upon me as we shared our lives with each other. We also had passionate debates about the political narratives in Northern Ireland. It was obvious that our political thinking had been shaped by our upbringing. Our stories moulded us and it was wonderful to realise that my story was not diminished by someone else's story but enriched by it. Our inherited narratives may have been different, but together they formed a richer, bigger picture. This was true politically as well as from the perspective of our faith stories.

Some of our politics lectures were at 2.00 p.m., a very difficult time to concentrate as it is just after lunch. Brendan and I shared notes from these lectures as we usually dozed off at different times, so between us we were able to cover the bits we had missed! I think it is fair to say this was simpler for me as his handwriting was easier to decipher than mine. We also decided to visit each other in our religious contexts. I found myself at Mass in the Catholic chaplaincy at Queen's on Ash Wednesday, when everyone else received ashes on their forehead and the sacrament of bread and wine. It was a very meaningful liturgy, as we were reminded of the scriptural truth that we will all return to ashes. There was a sadness that I could not receive the sacrament, but this is a reminder of how the need for dialogue between the churches is critical. In remembering the pain of separation, we can be inspired to pray for the visible unity that is God's gift in the midst of our human divisions.

Brendan then had the opportunity to join me at a Christian Union meeting. At those meetings there was no liturgy and worship was usually a song or hymn and a prayer. The meeting was organised around an invited speaker, who would speak on a chosen subject. It was essentially a lecture using scripture to explain and unpack the matter in hand. The programme was planned for the term and the title of each address was known in advance. I have no recollection of the subject the evening Brendan came with me to a meeting. However, I do remember it was not very inspiring; in fact, it was rather dull.

It is one of the tendencies of this type of meeting that those listening are given a great deal of information, but I found myself experiencing what I can only describe as 'spiritual indigestion'. In reading the gospel accounts I am always fascinated by how Jesus told stories and did not explain them, except for the parable of the sower. I believe he wanted us to wrestle with the parables and discern from the Spirit how we could interpret them for our own daily lives. It was our responsibility to respond and live out his teaching. The cerebral world I so often experienced in a Protestant culture left me dissatisfied. 'Jesus seems more interested in stirring curiosity than in completely satisfying it – in making people hungry and thirsty for more rather than making them feel complacently stuffed.'[3]

During my three years at Queen's I was struggling with a nagging sense of being called to ordained ministry. In truth, I was trying to resist, avoid and run away from this call. My experience of church as a child and my mother's pain caused by the church made this all the more confusing. Conversations with Brendan were helpful as he understood the magnitude of such a calling. He also grasped the implications of the necessary commitment to this way of life.

The Church of Ireland chaplain at Queen's when I was there was the Reverend John Dinnen. We had many conversations about ordination and he challenged my struggle with the Church. He told me to read the New Testament letters and see if I could find the perfect church. With his typical dry wit, he was pointing me to the reality that the Church has always been a collection of broken people. It is not perfect and cannot be because of people like me. Slowly, but surely, my defences were worn down and I felt I must at least pursue this call further.

My local parish was supportive of my call; my close friends appeared to be more sure than I was. My mum was quiet on the matter and just wanted me to be certain. There were two members of my small departmental prayer group who took me for coffee to try and dissuade me from this journey. They could not understand how God could be calling me to ministry in the Church of Ireland as there was a 'paper-thin wall' between it and the Roman Catholic Church. Suspicion and religious division run very deep in Northern Ireland and it is difficult at times to find people dispensing grace. The saddest part of this moment was that it was done out of a genuine care for me and my spiritual well-being.

I attended a selection conference in Dublin a few months after my twentieth birthday. This was an affirming and positive experience. Within a few weeks of the conference, Bishop George Quin, my sponsoring bishop, informed me that I had been accepted for training, dependent on finishing my degree at Queen's. I graduated in July the following year and I started training in the Divinity Hostel in Dublin that September. I was a student living away from home and was enrolled in Trinity College Dublin to study for ordination.

The ordinands stayed in the Divinity Hostel and this meant I had a single room, shared toilet and bathroom. We all ate together in a formal dining room. There were other students staying in the hostel who were not training for ordination and this made for a healthy environment. The rhythm of the day for ordinands was organised around three services in chapel: before breakfast, before dinner and at 9.00 p.m. There was a rota for all ordinands to lead the liturgy and read the scriptures of the day. On Saturdays and Sundays there was the same rhythm, but attendances were not as good! On Wednesday evenings and Sunday mornings there was a Eucharist. It was in essence a seminary with a monastic routine of eating, study and prayer. This was part of the formation for ministry.

I had just finished unpacking and was walking down the corridor towards the chapel when I met the sub-warden, Canon Jim Hartin, talking with another student. Jim introduced me to Peter Barrett and told us we would become good friends. We laughed – and yet how profoundly true Jim's words would prove. We shared those years of training, and his friendship was a special gift. Our different backgrounds and faith stories were to bring insights and gifts for the journey ahead. My difficulty with church from my childhood was tempered by Peter's love of church. The strong Protestant influences of Northern Ireland were softened by Peter's southern openness and acceptance of others.

There was a moment during the first term in Divinity Hostel that cemented our friendship. Peter kept telling me during that first term that his father wanted to meet me as he knew my paternal grandparents. My father disappeared when I was six and his problems appeared to have deepened when his parents died. This was during the first three years of my life so I did not know them. I was intrigued to meet someone who could shed light on my family history. We borrowed a car on the last Wednesday of term and drove to Glenageary, a suburb of Dublin, to visit Alec Barrett. We spent three or four hours with him and it was fascinating. My grandparents had stayed in the Barrett family guest house in Dún Laoghaire before Peter's mother died. The Barretts had visited my grandparents' home in Hillhall, near Lisburn, and they had shared interests in pigeons and dogs. We came back to college on a high, but in the early hours of Thursday morning Peter knocked on my door to tell me his father had died during the night with a heart attack.

One of the lessons of this friendship was the ability to disagree without losing friendship. It was also enriching to learn from each other. This was something that I had not found in my formative church circles. All issues of faith and belief had a right or a wrong answer. There was no room for compromise or listening to other viewpoints. One of the most beautiful and painful moments of our friendship was when we sat together at a Church of Ireland Synod in 1990, when there was a vote to agree on the ordination of women to the priesthood and the episcopacy. Peter voted against and I voted for – a painful moment for us both as the disagreement was profound.

Friendship is a special gift. It is wonderful to discover Jesus in people we disagree with, but this is more likely when we have a bond of friendship that helps us look beyond difference. Too often friendships are not formed because there are assumptions and religious labels that keep us apart. It is through relationships that we can find alternative ways of knowing and loving the same Jesus. This friendship lasted a lifetime until Peter's sudden death, also with a heart attack, in 2015.

Peter was a very good hockey player, having represented Leinster and Ireland at different levels. He managed to persuade me to train with the hockey club and I found a new respect for hockey players. The rigour of this training was much greater than anything I had experienced at football training. The sprints were particularly difficult, partly because they were at the beginning and end of training. He managed to get me on a hockey pitch once, but I could not get used to not kicking the ball – and it was very hard and too small!

As part of our training we also paid visits to Maynooth College, Co. Kildare, where students were trained for priesthood in the Roman Catholic Church. It was a large seminary in a delightful location. The chapel is beautiful and inspiring. Meeting fellow students studying for ordination was particularly important for me with my cultural background, and it proved formative. The journey of the students I met and shared stories with was much more difficult than mine. They were entering a world of celibacy and the cost of following their vocation looked much greater than mine in the world I was moving towards. We shared meals, worship and even a beer.

There was also great fun in this ecumenical engagement. The Seminaries League gave the opportunity for different colleges to play football against each other. We had a good team and I enjoyed the thrill of playing football again. However, it is fair to say that most of the opposition teams were not natural football players. There was a rough and tumble to these games, and it was important to avoid being tackled by some of our opponents, who were not used to the speed and agility of the game. It was a real test of ecumenical relations, but we more than survived and had a good time.

Dublin was a wonderful place to be a student. It was amazing that a city only one hundred miles south of Belfast could be so different. I was not being searched entering shops, there were no bomb scares, there were no troops walking the streets, and I could leave Trinity any time and cycle back to the hostel. The freedom was all the more special because of the contrast with Belfast and my Queen's experience. There were those from my own church background who were concerned about me living in Dublin, and there was suspicion and even hostility towards the south of Ireland. I had discovered that there were many unhelpful and dangerous assumptions about the other in the divided community of Northern Ireland, so it was interesting to experience the vibrant and fascinating world of being a student in Trinity. It was great fun to be able to cycle back to my accommodation late at night and stop for some chips on the way home.

The main reason for me being there was to study and prepare for ordination, but I did enjoy the demands of studying theology. I quickly discovered that it was a subject that allowed me to flourish. The uncertainty, mystery and difficult questions gave me space to pursue subjects that fascinated me. I do not believe that faith is about certainty but about discovering that questions, and not answers, deepen faith. The certainties that had been part of my religious experience were being questioned and stretched. I found this stimulating and it made me wrestle with my own faith and enjoy the questions rather than always wanting answers.

On this journey of faith I have discovered that the pious answers we are offered are frequently unhelpful. So often we try to answer questions people are not asking. When we offer religious platitudes to counter their struggle or pain, in fact we are denying the struggle and insulting the pain. 'There are a certain number of religious people who come into each conversation armed with a set of off-the-shelf maxims and bumper-sticker sayings. Instead of actually listening to the questions from the people in front of them, they just unfurl the maxims regardless of circumstances.'4

The pattern of daily worship was at times difficult to maintain, but it did give a form and shape to daily prayers. In all the services there were psalms and readings from scripture. It was only after ordination that I discovered the value of the daily office. The discipline and structure were important, especially in the busyness of parish life. Silence and contemplation, however, were my main source of help on my journey of faith. I also learned the value of symbols and signs as we worshipped together. Candles and crosses in churches were frowned upon in my church background. They were treated with disdain and suspicion as they were part of Roman Catholic worship.

It was Robert, or Bob, who helped me see the beauty of candles, a reminder that the light of Christ has never been extinguished. They also point us to the numinous; the mystery of faith. We cannot contain our faith by words only, we need symbols and gestures to remind us that God is God and not our 'best mate'. One of the joys in my time in college was to prepare chapel for worship, including lighting the candles. This was a new world for me that I have enjoyed and cherished ever since. Listening to the stories and faith journeys of others has always helped me grow in my understanding and enriched my journey. It has also challenged and disturbed me at times – and that has been invaluable.

I was a member of the Christian Union in Trinity, but it was very different from Queen's. The group was much smaller and more diverse. The friendships established there were particularly important because it was healthy to have friends outside the confined world of ordination training. The meetings took place on a Saturday evening and this also meant there were social gatherings afterwards. This was to lead to the most important moment of my time in Trinity. It was there that I first met Liz, who was to become my soulmate, best friend and wife. Over the years I have come to realise how incredibly special it has been to have her – and our children (and their families) – on this journey with me. Ministry and leadership is a lonely place and I admire, respect and pray for those who have to do it on their own.

I was very fortunate to experience student life in two different settings. The friends I made have been friends for life and the lessons learned have shaped and influenced me since. My faith was stretched and challenged, and it strengthened and developed in response. The easy, trite answers of my youth gave way to a love of questions. A faith that is safe and secure within set boundaries was never my spiritual home and I discovered that the faiths and journeys of others can enrich and teach me. The faith of others is not a threat, but is there to show me that this jewel of faith, received as a gift, has many facets I have still to taste and see.

JIM > In the Wilderness

The results of my A levels were good – not great, but good; good enough to be the first person in my family to gain a place at university. It came with a huge sense of pressure for me, I remember. The pressure came from a number of sources. Some of these sources were external and some were internal. The internal ones were my own anxious inner child, who liked to remind me (and tries to remind me to this day) that I will not measure up and that the world out there will devour me. I suppose, at this middle stage of my life and with the benefit of hindsight, I can see that this inner pressure, this anxious inner child, was a manifestation of a number of the outer pressures. I can see how I internalised both my parents' hopes and aspirations for me, and their anxieties about 'letting me go' out into the world. This paradoxical stance of simultaneously being exhilarated that I was to be educated, and therefore spend a considerable amount of time outside the little island of West Belfast that I had grown up in, and fearing that this might put me at terrible risk of meeting some violent end, made for a heady mix of emotions that I did not at all understand or cope with well. I should give you a spoiler alert here: this part of my story does not end happily for the Jim of 1990 to 1993. The older Jim I am now can see the arc of the story, the purpose of the journey, the presence of Jesus with me through those times. The young Jim, not so much. But I digress …

And so, in October 1990, I got on a bus to travel from the western corner of Belfast across the city centre I so much enjoyed walking through on Saturday afternoons, and on to the south of Belfast and, with it, university land. I was like a rabbit caught in the headlights. All of the sights and sounds, the diverse mix of people and the even more diverse range of nightlife, were like a drug to me. And quickly I was under its spell. I remember the feeling of coming from what felt like a very small world and landing in this very big world. And as many small-time boys and girls do, I lost my way, and fairly quickly.

I had decided to study history and social anthropology. I chose these subjects even though they were not my passion. My passion had always been for drama, music, writing and helping people. But these subjects were shunned and looked down upon in the grammar school I had attended. They might be a nice hobby but one could never make one's living successfully in those fields – that was the message I was roundly given, both at school and at home. And so, not for the first or last time in my life, I was about to be taught a very valuable and costly lesson – my passions are God-given. I have passions for a reason, and that reason has always turned out to be for the greater good. My experience at Queen's University was to be one of wilderness, because not only had I not followed my passions, but I began to re-evaluate my life choices. I concluded, now that I was in this world of university lectures and late-night parties, that I did not really need what had been a comfort and anchor to me in life heretofore – my religion. I stopped going to Mass very quickly after I started attending Queen's. Well, in the circles I was beginning to hang out in, religion was a joke at best, sinister at worst. In my heart

I knew that was not how I felt, but I was drawn along in the wake of this secular tide. Indeed, I became part of the sea that tide rose in. But it cost me. I was often conflicted in my thoughts and emotions.

One event always resides to the fore of my memories of that time. I had gone to the Student Union on a Friday night to meet friends, have a drink and dance the night away to the 1960s music that had such a resurgence in the late 1980s and early 1990s. I fell in love with Jimi Hendrix and Cream. I listened to Neil Young and Buffalo Springfield every day. Truth be told, I had become something of a hippy! And so, that Friday night, with my flared trousers and suede coat, I went to dance and feel carefree. Or so I thought ...

On my way to the bathroom at some stage during the night I met a young man and woman, perhaps a year or two above me. They were handing out religious tracts and speaking to anyone who would stop. To be fair, not many people were stopping. When they caught my eye and smiled, I stopped with them. I have never been a person to ignore or walk by someone who wants to talk. The conversation began with some pleasantries about the night and the music blaring out from the hall, but quickly turned to religion. The young people were from a Protestant background and asked a question like, 'Do you know Jesus as your saviour?' Here was me, a hippy fall-away from Catholic West Belfast. The whole idea of talking of Jesus in this way was totally alien to me. It had never been the language of my upbringing and I didn't know how to respond. I told them so. They asked me to come sit with them and I did. We talked for about half an hour, as I remember, and even as I write this I feel the ache I felt that night. It was a kind of pull inside me. I knew these two people had a deep faith and I knew that I wasn't being true to mine. That hurt and shamed me. And yet their language, their tradition and their invitation were ones that I just couldn't move towards fully at that time. Bear in mind that I had never knowingly spoken to a Protestant person in my life until I had started at Queen's just a half a year or so before this encounter. I was lost in the conversation, to be honest, and I was unhappy in my life. I had concluded fairly quickly that I did not have a great future in history and anthropology. I was less interested in the habits of the Trobriand islanders and the history of political liberalism than I was in just surviving this unhappy time. And so, with an ache in my gut still, I thanked the young people and went back to the hall to dance the night away.

The conversation stuck with me, however. What was it saying to me? Back then, it just felt like it had shamed me – not that they had shamed me, but that I had felt ashamed of myself. And, powerless to do anything about it (shame always disempowers and is not what God desires), I did as St Peter does in John chapter 21 when he found himself not knowing how to do what God was asking of him. Peter went back to the old ways by saying, 'I'm going fishing.' I went back to the old ways by saying, 'I'm not going to bother with God or religion and I will just party on!' For me, just as for Peter, God had a lesson in store and a desire to see me return.

That return took time and did not happen at Queen's. Indeed, my time there, as I have said above, was an unhappy one. I was living at home and travelling through the war-torn streets of what we now know were the last few bitter years of the Troubles before the ceasefires first came in 1994.

This backdrop of violence took its toll on me back then. It dictated my choice of bus route – would I go down the Donegall Road to Queen's or through town? The Donegall Road bus was quicker but it meant that I had to travel across the dividing line between Catholic West Belfast and Protestant South Belfast. The bus was attacked with stones from time to time and, depending on other violence that was taking place, choosing that bus might be dangerous. Looking back now, and considering my own children who are in their late teens and twenties, I can see how that pressure and stress contributed to my feeling so much in the wilderness at that time. It was awful what we did to each other and how we allowed ourselves to be led into division based on myth.

Living at home meant that I didn't fully commit to the student experience. I had one foot in two camps, if you like. The lightness and party atmosphere of university land was contrasted with what, in memory, always feels like the cold and dark atmosphere of my home district in West Belfast. Being of university age also meant that I came under more scrutiny from the security forces who patrolled the streets around where I lived. This, in turn, led to experiences that were both frightening and enlightening. Allow me to share two such experiences.

'You're an IRA scumbag!'

I can still hear the soldier's high-pitched scream and smell his tobacco breath as he yelled into my face.

'You're an IRA scumbag and we're going to get you all!'

He was losing it completely. I think he threw his rifle down, but I can't be sure. I was frozen with fear and it caused my peripheral vision to become somewhat foggy. I could only focus on his face and, in particular, his mouth. It snarled at me with pure venom.

One minute earlier I had been walking down the Glen Road with my friend talking about … well, what nineteen-year-old boys in Belfast talked about at that time: girls, music, girls, football, girls. Our journey took us past the local RUC station, which was heavily fortified and replete with military presence. The presence on that particular day included soldiers from the Parachute Regiment. As we were walking past the station, a patrol of soldiers emerged onto the street. When soldiers came out of the station they ran out quickly – having ascertained that they were easy targets for gunmen until they got well away from the gates and into the streets for cover from buildings and/ or people. So out they ran. Nothing strange in that. My friend and I didn't bat an eyelid. We continued walking. However, soon we saw that one of the young soldiers (it's only now in hindsight that I see that he was young; at the time, he was an adult and I was a child) was making a beeline for us. We stood still because we knew, even at that young age, that to move away would be a foolish thing to do.

And so it was that he came up to us and began screaming into our faces, telling us that we were IRA scumbags and that he intended to 'get' us. My friend and I knew that we were not in the IRA. We were not convinced, however, that he knew or, to be fair, that he even cared. He had the look of a man winding up to do some violence. I remember looking round at one point for help. I saw adults in the local shop doorways and across the street. They had all stopped to see what the noise was. They saw us two boys being yelled at by this armed man, while his armed mates stood watching as well. They did nothing. I remember a fleeting thought entering my mind: Why are they not helping us? It came and it went. I had other things to think about.

The soldier continued to rant and call down all sorts of curses on our heads. He regaled us with tales of what he was going to do to 'all you IRA scumbags'. In the face of this tirade, I could do nothing but wish it was over and pray that he did not follow through on his threats. As it turns out, he didn't. He blew himself out and walked away.

No one batted an eyelid. His soldier friends simply walked away with him. The adults who had been watching began to get on with whatever it was they had been doing before the noise interrupted them. For that had been all it was – noise. Noise in a conflict that had brought far worse than noise. No shots here, no wounds, no blood and no death. All else was just noise. It didn't really matter. Unless you were subject to it, I guess.

My friend and I were pale-faced, shocked and relieved. We moved on. We probably laughed about it. We definitely didn't feel like it had been a laughing matter. We didn't speak of it again. There were other incidents that took its place as time went on.

I look back on this incident now with the benefit of some thirty years and more on the clock. I'm no longer nineteen years old. In fact, my children are all that age or older now. The thought of them being bullied on the street in the way I was is quite distressing. The thought of witnessing anyone else's child being bullied in that way is also distressing. Putting myself back there as an adult, would I have acted differently from those adults who stood by and didn't intervene? Maybe not. They knew that the soldier was more likely to hurt an adult intervening than the children in front of him. Still, would I have said something? In the comfort of my middle-aged fantasy mind, I would have. Maybe …

And what of the soldier? I have thought about him over the years. He was one of a few individual soldiers I remember. He has occupied different spaces in my mind over the years. Early on, I was angry at him – scandalised, even. How could he have done what he did? What else did he do?

As time has gone on, though, and as I have grown older than he would have been then, I think about him differently. What was going through his mind that day? What had he been through already? What did he fear he would go through? These guys had seen all sorts of mayhem in other countries as well as our own by that stage. As he burst out of that RUC station, did he see the enemy all round him? I think he did. Poor young fella.

This is a very complex place we live in, full of competing histories and stories of fear, hurt and death. We owe it to the current generation to end what we can and to begin a new chapter where we can.

There should be no more young men bursting out into our streets with guns, seeing nothing but the enemy all around. There should be no more young people bullied on our streets by armed men – from wherever they come. There should be no acceptance of any level of violence against the young or old of our land. And yet, that was the backdrop to my university experience. No matter where I was in leafy South Belfast, I knew that I was going home to experiences like this.

However, not all my encounters with the British army were like this. And, indeed, it is funny the things you notice when someone is standing in front of you with a gun.

On the particular occasion I will relate now (because there were many), I noticed three things. First, this person was about the same age as me. Second, he looked really pissed off. Third, and I don't know why I looked at his hands – oh yeah, he was carrying a gun that was pointed kinda in my direction – I noticed that he had tattoos across his knuckles.

In a dark street in the middle of Turf Lodge, working my way home from a friend's house nearby, it wasn't unusual to be stopped by a patrol of British soldiers. Since I was about fourteen I had been stopped several times per week. Mostly, it was a perfunctory conversation about who I was and where I was going. Sometimes the soldiers were even quite polite. Sometimes. I had long since stopped being anxious about this. I didn't feel much at all about it, really. It was part of existence in this part of the world. And to be honest, I had switched off.

So, when I was stopped by this particular patrol and was questioned by this particular soldier, I suppose my mind wandered a little and settled on his tattoos. In the middle of the mini interrogation under the street lights, I asked the soldier about his tattoos.

'You like Pink Floyd?'

'What?'

'Your tattoos. Do you like Pink Floyd?'

I waited to gauge his reaction to me turning the tables and asking him questions. Experience had shown me that not many of these soldier guys wanted any sort of civil or personal conversation to ensue from our encounters. But, ever the optimist, and never the violent type, I gave it a go.

'Yeah.' Eloquent response. I'll go a bit further, I thought. 'Cool, man.' I matched his eloquence with my recently acquired hippy speak.

'You?'

'Yeah.' I laboured the word as if to add emphasis and let him know that I really did like Pink Floyd. This, unfortunately, was a wee white lie. I didn't not like Pink Floyd. In fact, I had had a sense for many years up to that point that I should like Pink Floyd (like hippy speak, I had also recently acquired hippy hair and hippy clothes). I just didn't really know much of their music. I had heard some of it and broadly liked it. So while my lie to the soldier was indeed a lie, it was only a white lie. And, given the context, it facilitated an easier conversation than could have been the case. So, yay Pink Floyd!

Thankfully he didn't ask me to name any of their songs or albums. Instead:

'What else you into?'

For the next few minutes we traded bands and songs we liked. We both relaxed into this conversation and, bizarre as it sounds, I think we both enjoyed talking to each other. It turned out he was the same age as me: nineteen.

'What are you doing over here, man?' This question could go wrong.

He had a faraway look of sadness in his eyes now.

'I don't want to be here. I hate it here. I don't really want to be a solider at all.'

'Then why are you? A solider, I mean.'

'Have you GCSEs or A levels?' he asked.

I had both and told him that I had started university.

'Well, I don't have any qualifications. I was rubbish at school. Came out with nothing. Couldn't get a job. I'd been on the dole for ages. I was pissing my life away. So, it was either join up or stay on the dole. So, I joined up. And ended up here.'

I didn't know what to say to him. I didn't know his whole story, but I could see that he had a limited number of choices in life and he made the best one he could. And ended up here. Belfast. Most of my friends who came from Belfast didn't want to be in Belfast in 1991. So I could imagine coming here wasn't the best experience in the world.

There was a cough from one of his soldier friends who had been watching our conversation evolve. He seemed to speak fluent cough, because the body language of my soldier changed. He stood more erect. He looked over at one of his mates (someone further up the chain of command, I imagine), then at me.

'See ya.' He moved off, gun in hand, scanning the street around him.

Unhappy in Belfast, 1991.

I walked home and, in the ten minutes it took me to do so, I didn't think much of our meeting. I had other things to deal with in life. I was young. I was lucky to have opportunities that many didn't. But this conversation stayed with me. Every time I see a person with tattoos on their knuckles, it reminds me of that young lad I met in Turf Lodge. Whatever happened to him? I hope his tour of Belfast was uneventful – for him and for those he encountered.

My own 'tour' of university came to an abrupt end in 1993 when, with only a few months to go, I became so unhappy and so convinced that the course I was studying, and the course my life was taking, were wrong, that I dropped out. I was now not only in the wilderness, but I was also a failure, or so I told myself. Shame stung me again. Little did I know that God was in that mess with me. Little did I know that God was shepherding me, yes, even in the parties and the walking away from my prayers and religious practice. Even in my mistakes and in my bad behaviour and treating people poorly, as I did from time to time. Even then, God was there. And little did I know that this experience of wilderness and being on the outside would engender in me a new passion for loving and being with people on the margins of society and finding wisdom and beauty when I encountered them.

When I left university and went into the world of work, I began to scent out God's call to another way of living.

REFLECTION

Alan and Jim have highlighted the following issues in this chapter:

1. The importance of meeting the other in the context of myth and suspicion
2. Faith and the importance of questions rather than answers
3. The importance of late adolescence and early adulthood in forming our world view

Reflect
In what ways do you see these challenges in your own life experience?

Challenge
Having read these reflections, in what ways do you hear God challenging you to discover Jesus in the other?

Pray
John 18:37-39
Matthew 18:10

NOTES

1. McAleese, *Here's the Story*, p. 92.
2. John 13:34-35 in Eugene Peterson (transl.), *The Message: The Bible in Contemporary Language*, Colorado Springs, CO: NavPress, 2002, p. 1949.
3. Brian D. McLaren, *The Secret Message of Jesus: Uncovering the Truth That Could Change Everything*, Nashville, TN: Thomas Nelson, 2006, pp. 206–7.
4. David Brooks, *The Second Mountain: The Quest for a Moral Life*, London: Allen Lane, 2019, p. 35.

CHAPTER FOUR
Grief, Segregation and Nudges of the Spirit

ALAN > A Different World

It was a bright summer evening and my world was about to change forever. I wore my new clerical shirt and my bright shiny collar for the first time and it unnerved me. I was ordained deacon in Down Cathedral on 24 June 1981 by Bishop Robin Eames. During my last few months in college there had been a process, for all those being ordained, to decide where they would serve their first three years of ministry as a curate assistant. I was assigned to St Elizabeth's, Dundonald. I had spent the first four years of my family life living in Dundonald with my paternal grandparents and I had been baptised in this church. I felt somewhat like a prodigal son returning home.

This was a thriving and busy parish. It had a strong history and identity as conservative and evangelical. The rector I worked with was relatively new to the parish and I was the first curate that he had chosen. As this was my background, I felt this was where I belonged. However, in my time there I began to realise that I had many questions about religious identity and practice that I needed to disentangle.

One of the attractions of this large parish was its active and developing youth ministry. There was a very gifted team of leaders and a clear focus on discipleship and worship, encouraging gifts and mutual support. The leaders were shaped by charismatic experiences and this in itself led to tension with some in the parish, including the rector. One of the key lessons for me was that of loyalty to my rector. His theological outlook disagreed with the influence of the charismatic strand of church life to which I was open and receptive, but he was the boss.

In my first few months another difficult issue arose that left me asking questions about my principles in ministry. The Troubles were at their height and many local Protestant churches had strong links with the Orange Order. The rector wanted me to take a service for the local lodge, but after my experiences of watching my Roman Catholic neighbours being burnt out of their homes and their church being desecrated, I was struggling. I had thought about this issue during my training and had decided that I would rather not take any of these services. I could not accept or affirm the Orange Order's faith that excluded Roman Catholics. My rector did not agree with my thinking, but gave me the space to decline, and I was grateful for his support.

One of the roles that I was given while in this parish was to help in the chaplaincy of the Ulster Hospital. I found this stimulating, challenging and enriching. This was a team chaplaincy shared with clergy from the other main denominations. The sharing of friendship, stories and our faith journeys was a wonderful gift. The role involved visiting patients who had allegiance with the Church of Ireland and informing their local clergy. However, I often met people from different churches and from none. There was also the opportunity to support and encourage the staff, whose service to others was an inspiration.

In parish ministry the pace at which things had to be done was at times relentless. There was the frustration of rarely being able to finish anything. The sudden shift in emotions was also strange – moving from birth to death in minutes. The trust that was given to me was staggering. People would tell me their life stories, their hopes, their fears, and share with me deeply personal thoughts.

There were many difficult and painful moments but I was given the privilege of sharing in people's lives at their most vulnerable and hurting, particularly when death visited a family. The raw pain of death and grief is excruciating for the bereaved. Words are inadequate and religious clichés insult the pain, but my presence and listening were valued. I learned so much from the families I was meant to be serving. Observing acts of kindness and love was both humbling and challenging.

The parish of Dundonald had grown as many from Belfast escaped to the new housing in various estates built in the area. As people moved to these houses they also brought with them their experiences of the conflict. There were those who had had to flee their homes or had been burnt out of them. In many of these new estates there was a deep anger at the continuing violence of the IRA. This anger and resentment were never very far below the surface and could erupt at any moment. I had been in the parish nearly six months when I witnessed one such incident.

The Reverend Robert Bradford was a Methodist minister and a Vanguard Unionist and Ulster Unionist Member of Parliament for the South Belfast constituency. He was shot dead by the IRA in a community centre in Finaghy, Belfast, while hosting a political surgery. The caretaker in the centre, Kenneth Campbell, a Protestant, was also killed in the attack. Reverend Bradford's funeral was held in Dundonald Presbyterian Church and led by a good friend of his, the Reverend Roy Magee. I was in the crowd outside the church and the anger was palpable and ferocious. The Secretary of State, Jim Prior, attended the funeral, and as he arrived with his security detail he was jostled and people called, 'You're a killer!' When he left the church some of the crowd were trying to overturn his car, but the security forces managed to get him away safely. Emotions in this beautiful country run very deep and they cannot always be controlled. These events were deeply disturbing. A public servant gunned down, a caretaker killed, a funeral disrupted by angry crowds, and all done in the name of politics – yet with religious labels attached. Families are left devastated by a grief that never goes away.

It is stating the obvious to say that the background to these early years in ministry was the ongoing violence and horror of the Troubles. As part of my role I did marriage preparation. I remember meeting a young couple one Monday evening in the church office to plan their wedding. The hymns were chosen, the readings selected and the legal requirements carefully explained. Constable Thomas John Bingham has been looking forward to his wedding and future family life. In an instant both were taken away from him. A thousand-pound landmine was detonated as he was travelling in an unmarked police car along with Sergeant William Ritchie Savage.

The world would never be the same for his fiancée, family and friends. Those who loved him faced into an abyss. I spent time with his family and was amazed at their determination to celebrate his life, but their grief is a pain they have had to live with ever since, as do the family and friends of Sergeant Savage.

I will never forget his funeral: the sombre tones of the RUC band and the guard of honour by his colleagues; the procession of local politicians as they made sure they were caught on camera on the way into the service; the array of television cameras and the swarm of journalists. These tragic family moments of grief were in the media spotlight. My focus was on his fiancée and family, whose hearts were breaking in such a public place. After the service, Constable Bingham was buried in St Elizabeth's graveyard.

For those who loved him this was not an end, but the beginning of a lifetime of loss and grief. I was able to continue to walk with them, but I will never understand their loss. However, I had to face some difficult questions in terms of my discovering Jesus in the other. The violence that pushed our communities further apart in Northern Ireland was on our television screens every day. I had seen it up close and was angry at how a fellow human being could cause such pain to other human beings and their families. Violence begets violence, and I have always found it impossible to accept the rationale of those who try to justify their violent actions. It is true that if we take a tooth for a tooth and an eye for an eye, then everyone will end up toothless and blind.

Deep within me there was still an anger at those who sought to shape our future with violence. This violence was then returned with interest, and this was a path leading nowhere but to the graveyards of our country. Inherent in this trajectory was the lazy assumption that every Roman Catholic was linked to terrorism and that every Protestant was prepared to resort to violence in response. Ministering to my community was made more difficult by the suspicion and hurt caused by cruel acts of violence perpetrated by defenders of their cause:

> Tribalism seems like a way to restore the bonds of community. But it is actually the dark twin of community. Community is connection based on mutual affection … Community is based on common humanity; tribalism on common foe. Tribalism is always erecting boundaries and creating friend/enemy distinctions. Mistrust is the tribalist world-view.[1]

Deep within me was a desire, formed by my teenage experiences, to reach beyond the tribal walls of this beautiful province. It appeared to me, as I continued in ministry, that part of my calling was not what everyone wanted.

While I was serving in Dundonald I received the opportunity to do some broadcasting with Downtown Radio. I was invited to write and record 'Just a Moment', a daily religious slot that was broadcast during the early-morning show. It was a short thought for the day in the midst of music, news and banter from the hosts. This was something I thoroughly enjoyed and eventually it would lead to me becoming the Church of Ireland adviser to Downtown Radio. It was also a great reminder that, to communicate in this or in any medium, storytelling and painting word pictures were critical.

It was in this setting that I first encountered the Reverend Father Gerry Patton, one of the best storytellers I ever met. He won an award for one of his early-morning slots in which he described sitting with his father in a Belfast pub and watching the barman pour a pint of Guinness. You could almost taste the Guinness! The engineers in the station often asked for it to be broadcast again. He will reappear later in these reflections when our paths cross again in a different setting.

While still in my final year in Dublin, I had met my soulmate and best friend, and it was at the end of my second year of ministry that we were married. Liz began her medical career as a junior doctor and life became even more busy, but fulfilling. I could not have survived ministry without her support and love. One year later, we moved to another ministry where I joined a team led by Canon Brian Mayne. This was in a rural setting with seven small parishes and we lived in Ardglass. From the study in our new home the view was spectacular, looking towards the Mourne Mountains and Dundrum Bay, with Coney Island in the foreground.

Brian encouraged me to enrol for some further study and it was refreshing to be studying part-time while serving in a parish. I spent just over two years in this team and I found the experience renewing and enriching. It was a very different setting from Dundonald, partly because it was rural, but also because it was predominantly nationalist and Catholic. This gave me much more scope to seek to cross the divide and develop ecumenical relationships.

When we moved into Ardglass the parish priest was very ill, and he died a few months later. The parochial house and church were just opposite the rectory where we lived. He died on Maundy Thursday and his funeral mass was on Easter Day in the afternoon. I informed my rector I would like to go and he encouraged me to do so to represent the local parish community. The welcome I received was overwhelming. I was invited to sit at the front and was also asked to read a scripture. Bishop Cahal Daly was presiding at the Mass and he welcomed me very warmly. The local Catholic community were genuinely appreciative of my presence. I saw this as a simple Christian gesture of prayerful presence and support. However, in the context of the Troubles and the community suspicions, this was not how everyone interpreted my actions.

Over the next week I received a few anonymous phone calls accusing me of betrayal and being a 'Fenian lover'. They were not threatening, but certainly abusive. I did not recognise any of the voices and there were no BT services to check the numbers. They were intimidating calls and I assume they were meant to scare me – and they did for a few days. However, I had so much support from the local community that I was able to put this down to experience. The next chapter of my story was so fascinating that this moment was quickly forgotten, but it was a reminder of the very deep suspicion, mistrust and anger in this divided land. 'The name of Jesus, whose life and message resonated with acceptance, welcome, and inclusion, has too often become a symbol of elitism, exclusion and aggression.'[2]

It was some months later that a new parish priest arrived in Ardglass, and I called at the parochial house to welcome him. His greeting was very warm and welcoming and he proceeded to introduce himself. He told me that if I was from Malone I would call him William, if I was from the Shankill I would call him Billy, but as he was from the Falls he was called Liam. To understand this you need some local knowledge of Belfast. Malone is an area of big houses and reasonable incomes, the Shankill is a loyalist area and the Falls a nationalist one. We laughed and enjoyed our first cup of coffee together. Father Liam and I were to become colleagues and good friends.

We quickly established a routine of meeting regularly and this developed further when we both accepted the invitation to be chaplains to the local Royal Air Force camp in Bishopscourt. The decision by Father Liam to accept the invitation was greatly appreciated by the RAF. The underlying suspicion in the Catholic community of any British forces was understandable. If nothing else, Jim's account of his experience as a young Catholic illustrates this well. We visited the camp together and enjoyed the hospitality of the officers' mess. There was some surprise in the mess when people discovered that Father Liam was teetotal.

One of the thorniest issues in many local communities was inter-church marriage. In the context of Northern Ireland this meant a Protestant marrying a Catholic. Liam and I discussed this at length as it was a real issue in our local community. We thought it would be helpful if we would offer to visit the families of those wishing to be married. In my short time in Ardglass, there was one particular pastoral situation where we offered this support and even though it was challenging for us all, it proved helpful. I do believe it was a useful model and I found it an enriching experience. It also strengthened my conviction that when church and community leaders model mutual respect and trust, they can facilitate better understanding and healing in our divided community.

My mother was a great knitter, and on more than one occasion Liam commented how much he liked my Aran cardigan, the handiwork of my mum. When I told my mum about this, she set to work and produced a beautiful Aran cardigan for him. It was great fun watching his pleasure as he walked round the village in his cardigan, informing anyone who asked that it was knitted for him by a 'Prod'. These simple human acts of kindness helped build bridges of friendship and support across the divide.

In our more serious discussions, I was always impressed by his commitment to Jesus, the Church and the people of the parish where he served. His whole life was spent serving the poor and people in pain. Before Ardglass he had been in the parish of Twinbrook at the heart of an ardent nationalist community. He arrived in Ardglass exhausted, having given himself unstintingly to the community he served. He was the parish priest when the funeral of Bobby Sands took place in the parish church. There were many nuances to this moment in our history, and we shared in great depth our individual struggles with our tortured and beautiful land. Our friendship was special to me because of his wisdom, his humour, his humility and his own personal faith story. I was enriched and blessed by the sharing of our lives and ministry.

We accepted each other as made in the image of God – fellow disciples following a strange and demanding call. A place of friendship and trust was nurtured and was a gift I came to cherish. On my journey with Jesus I have found some beautiful people who have shared Jesus with me from a different religious and cultural background. Father Liam Mullan was someone who gave me a new window into the loveliness of Jesus and I will be forever grateful.

I was ordained in Down Cathedral, as I recounted at the beginning of this chapter, and I will conclude these reflections by returning to that beautiful building. My rector, Canon Brian Mayne, had had a very serious accident and needed emergency surgery, spending some time in intensive care. He had walked through a glass panel in a local shopping centre. It had cut some arteries – hence the emergency surgery. This happened just before a special ecumenical service to celebrate St Patrick's Day. The four main church leaders would be present. It was an afternoon service and the plan was for choral evensong to be sung by the rector and the choir. The director of music asked me to step up in place of the rector and, after intensive training, I managed to be the cantor for this special act of worship. In the vestry before the service, Bishop Robin Eames informed our guests about what had happened and he thanked me for being willing to step into the breach. The cathedral was full and everything went as planned. I was very relieved when it was over. A few days later, I received a brief letter from Cardinal Tomás Ó Fiaich, the Roman Catholic archbishop and Primate of All Ireland. He thanked me for singing so well in such difficult circumstances. That is a letter I treasured from someone who represented the other community in Northern Ireland.

The next chapter of ministry was beginning to loom large on the horizon and it was very unsettling. I met various parish nominators to discuss the possibility of becoming their rector, but my concern with the Orange Order and their acts of worship was a stumbling block for some parishes. Liz and I were beginning to think about other options, such as parishes south of the border. However, the parish of Helen's Bay, through the bishop of the day, offered me the chance to become their rector. I will begin my reflections in the next chapter at that moment in my story.

I spent nearly six years as a curate, in two very different places. One of the gifts of parish ministry is the people; they shaped me and allowed me to make mistakes and to learn so much. In the context of these ramblings, it is the people from the other side of the road in religious terms that I want to recognise as helping me discover Jesus in the other. Rabbi Jonathan Sacks, in his insightful book *Celebrating Life*, pays tribute to his mother when he writes: 'By her example she taught me and my brothers what other, more overtly religious people often forget: that having faith in God means having faith in other people, and that the measure of righteousness lies in how many people we value, not in how many we condemn.'[3]

JIM > A Kind of Homecoming

I started working in a children's home in Belfast in March 1993. This came after I dropped out of university and spent a year or so working at a variety of jobs – including being a barman, a busker on the streets of Belfast, and a singer in nurseries for toddlers! It was a great time in many ways. I got to move outside of my own community more and see the city of Belfast from different angles. However, it was also a time of searching and wondering. What was I going to do? What was I going to be?

I had always felt drawn to helping people as a kind of vocation. I think this came from the combined messages my parents gave me growing up: people are good and, when they are in trouble, help if you can. These were good messages, I think. I know now, having heard about their childhoods and their struggles in life, that these messages derived from their own experience of needing others to help them as well as others needing their help. Both my parents lost parents when they were children. My mother lost her mother and my father lost his father. Sadly, both died of illnesses that, today, are easily treated and very unlikely to lead to death. Still, die they did – she at the tender age of twenty-five and he not much older at thirty-six. I suppose that, when they met, my parents had this loss in common and found solace in each other.

What they also had in common was an understanding of the power of helping others in times of great need. My mother's maternal aunt, the sister of my grandmother who died, took over maternal duties with my mother, who, because of this love and the love of her father, my grandfather, grew up with a sense of family and an experience of what it is to be lost and found again by love. My father's experience was different. He became the helper, and at the young age of twelve years old became the breadwinner for his mother and nine siblings. These were hard times; Belfast in the 1950s saw an overabundance of deficit. There were too many poor people and not enough opportunities to break free from the stranglehold of poverty. My dad, a child himself, walked the streets of Belfast selling sticks, doing odd jobs and scraping enough meagre earnings to put food on the table at home. While he encountered a lot of cruelty in his life at that time, he also encountered tremendous generosity. One example comes to mind.

In the late 1950s, one Christmas Day, my dad was on the street, looking to see if he could pick up any work from the local shops and houses, running errands. As he tells it, it was to be a day without Christmas dinner back home, never mind presents, which were a rarity at the best of times. These were not the best of times. Around 2.00 p.m., he was standing on the corner of the Crumlin Road and Tennent Street when a car pulled up and two older people got out. They approached my father and asked about him and what he was doing. Sensing that they 'had a few pounds', he told them of his plight in the hope that they might give him a shilling or two. To his surprise, they told him that they were Church of Ireland people and that they wanted to spend Christmas helping others, and invited him to their house for dinner. He readily agreed and he told me that he ate well and took enough food home later, when these kind folks dropped him back to where they had found him, for his family to eat as well. Quite amazing!

And so it was that my parents, having seen the love of God at work in their own struggles, encouraged me to be that presence of love and support when I could. Looking back, it is little wonder that I found employment in the helping professions. After the wilderness of my unhappy university career, taking up a job that seemed like a way to fulfil my vocation, my purpose, felt like a kind of homecoming.

And, indeed, it was a home that I went to work in – a children's home. It was situated in the south of the city and each day I crossed

Belfast from the west, into the centre, and off to the south. The children and families I worked with came from all over Northern Ireland. Many of their life stories were extremely distressing. Like my father's family back in the 1950s, poverty wreaked havoc on many of those I came into contact with. Along with many other staff, I tried to make life as comfortable and enjoyable as possible for the children in my care. I met some wonderful children and staff during the year or so that I worked there. My title was Residential Social Worker, although at that time I had no formal training in social work. That was to come a few years later.

They say that social work is a sort of secular priesthood; many of those who work in the field for any length of time bring an almost evangelical fervour to their work. I could see it in some of the staff around me. While religion was not a common topic of conversation in 'mixed' teams of people from different faith traditions (and none) in Northern Ireland at that time, I can see now how the committed and compassionate people I worked with then and later, when I qualified as a social worker, were what theologian Karl Rahner calls 'anonymous Christians'. His supposition was that a person, by living out a grace-filled life, working for the betterment of the world and the individuals in it, even when they don't identify as Christian, can be the presence of God's love, joy and mercy in the world. I met a lot of anonymous Christians, as well as overt Christians, in the realm of social work. In some way, I see myself as having been one of these anonymous Christians at this time as well. My practice of my faith, lost during university, had yet to return. However, the awakening in me of a heart for the hurt, the poor and the distressed was surely God's Spirit 'working in me', calling me home.

This was a period of important formation for me. I was learning how to meet, care for and understand people from wildly different backgrounds. I was being challenged to see good in people, even when they were behaving towards me in ways that were hurtful, both emotionally and physically. It was a time of testing and strengthening. As I reflect now, I can see how this time of my life was also shrouded in the stresses and strains of living in a divided society. The Troubles continued to rage around me, not only at home but also at work.

In and around May 1993, I was asked to hand-deliver a report to another building. One of the jobs of the staff in the home was to write reports about the young people for the plethora of meetings that were held with and/or about them. These reports were sent from the staff in the home to the children's social workers in the community. One such meeting was to be held and one such report was to be written and delivered. However, as sometimes happened, the children's home was very unsettled and the report was written too late for posting to the social services office. I was tasked with delivering it.

So, around half past ten that morning, I crossed the city from the south to the centre and then to the west. The social services office was in Cupar Street at the bottom of the Falls Road. Pre-ceasefire Falls Road could be a tense place. There were a lot of derelict buildings and signs of rioting and violence were carved into the roads and walls. The possibility of a Good Friday Agreement wasn't considered then by the vast majority of people, most of whom felt that violence would always be a feature of life in Northern Ireland. That morning on the Falls Road we were still firmly on a war footing.

When I arrived in Cupar Street I realised for the first time that I had no idea where the social services office actually was. I walked around for a bit but couldn't see any sign of it. I looked around for someone to ask but the street was deserted. It was eerily quiet. What to do? There were no mobile phones back then to phone the children's home. Would I knock on someone's door and ask?

Before I had time to decide, I saw someone else walk into the street – a man. I began to walk towards him. He was about the same height and build as me. He had shaggy brown hair and was wearing a dark outdoors jacket and a pair of jeans. He was walking perpendicular to me, having crossed into Cupar Street from elsewhere. I began to speak.

'Excuse me …'

No sooner had I spoken than he swung round to face me. He moved with great efficiency and I could see he was actually a lot stronger and fitter than me. As he spun around I saw that, by his side, he carried a pistol. I saw the black metal shape sitting very comfortably in his hand. I began to worry.

He didn't raise the gun. He didn't lose his cool. He looked me directly in the eye without showing any emotion at all. He studied me for a second or two. He seemed to be assessing me and the situation we found ourselves in. I couldn't move, rooted as I was to the spot in the deserted street. What was going to happen? Was this it? Was I to be another statistic?

The two seconds that I stood facing this man dragged on as if in slow motion. His assessment finished, he concluded that I didn't pose a threat to whatever he was doing and I was to be allowed to live. He turned on his heel and jogged back to where he came from. Again, he moved easily, with the bearing of a man who had trained for urban conflict. I watched as he rounded the corner and disappeared.

I let out a spluttering breath. I hadn't realised that I hadn't breathed since he'd spun round to face me. Moments later, as I stood still on the same spot, I heard sirens and saw four army jeeps coming up the street towards me. They rounded the same corner as my assessor and disappeared. The sirens stopped a few seconds later and I heard the vehicles halt for a short moment before opening and quickly closing their doors and speeding off again. My feeling is that I had encountered an undercover British soldier and, having encountered me, he radioed for his back-up to come and take him away. Perhaps I had stumbled upon an operation of some sort.

I was left shaken but, thankfully, otherwise unharmed. I stood rooted to the spot for a time, trying to settle myself. I couldn't shake off the look he had given me. At once cold and determined, it took me back to a childhood memory when I was an altar boy at the funeral of one of the ten Republican prisoners who died on hunger strike in 1981. One of the men came from my parish and his funeral cortège was accompanied up to the church steps (but not beyond) by a guard of honour consisting of around a dozen IRA men. As the cortège stopped at the steps, the priest and we altar boys came out to meet the coffin and receive the remains of the man into the church for the funeral rite. I found myself, for a short time, standing at the side of one of the IRA men who stood to attention at the side of the coffin. I looked up gingerly and saw his face through the netting he wore over his head to conceal his identity. He had that same steely look – cold and determined – that I saw later in 1993 in the face of the British soldier. The look scared me as a wee boy and it scared me as a young man. To be honest, the cold but determined look of men and women who can visit violence on others still scares me today.

During those awful last days, before some hope came in the form of the Belfast (Good Friday) Agreement in 1994, we witnessed tragedy that cut across our society. Three events later in 1993 brought home to me once again the futility of war and violence and the danger of the myth that we are different simply because of our faith tradition or claim on nationality.

On 23 October a bomb exploded on the Shankill Road in Belfast. Set on a faulty timer, it exploded prematurely, killing one of the IRA bombers and nine people going about their normal Saturday afternoon shopping. Our eyes drank in the news footage of yet another bombed-out building with yet more frantic searchers ripping through rubble for the dead and dying. Relatives screamed and cried and witnesses stood by, traumatised into a silent stare. As the names of the victims came to light, we heard of men, women and children having their lives ended and the hearts of their loved ones being ripped apart. And for what, we asked.

Three days later, in an act of the continual reprisal that the woefully named 'Troubles' became, a team of gunmen drove into the heart of the community where I lived (and still live) and raked a city council refuse site with gunfire, killing an old man I knew well and the brother of a school friend. Questioned about the pain inflicted by the bomb, the people controlling these gunmen cited revenge as their motive. We gathered at the site soon after for a prayer vigil and saw the scars that the bullets had left in the walls and windows of the site. As in the Shankill three days earlier, relatives shed tears and witnesses stood in silent horror at an act of sheer futility of the most vicious kind.

Then, on 30 October, another team of gunmen burst into the Rising Sun bar in Greysteel, County Derry, shouted 'trick or treat' in a display of twisted barbarism, and then shot everyone they could. They killed eight people – Protestant and Catholic, not that they cared – and wounded nineteen. The scene inside the bar was described later as 'hell-like'.

Hell-like. A good description of the place we were living in. Fear ruled and held an already fearful community in a tighter grip. Bars scrambled to get security systems in place, with buzzers and CCTV cameras being compulsory on the road where I lived. We feared another Greysteel. My friends and I decided that we wouldn't go into the city centre or the university area any more for a pint or to watch a band. We retreated into our own districts and battened down the hatches. My father insisted on driving me across the city to my work whenever he could, all to stop me travelling in and out of areas so ludicrously designated either 'us' or 'them'. The possibility of all-out civil war was once again the topic of conversations around dinner tables and in political parties.

Up until then I had fooled myself that my life was not really at risk. I had kidded myself that it always happened to others. All that ended in October 1993. It was then I realised, in some deep way that I had not allowed myself before, that the people who were dying were just like me. In the main they were going about living normal lives in the most abnormal of situations.

Where was God in all of this? Were we to be abandoned totally? At that point we didn't even dare to dream about the ceasefires that were to become a reality within a year. In October 1993, if you'd spoken to me in the language of peace, I'd have laughed at the suggestion. Or cried. Or both. Little did I know that good men and women were working so hard behind the scenes to deliver peace.

Back then I threw myself into my work of caring for the distressed and separated children in our care. And in so doing, I saw Jesus at work powerfully in the poor and struggling children and their families. At the time I would not have put that word on it – Jesus. No, I would have simply recognised their 'goodness', 'strength', 'love', 'commitment' – by-words for Jesus, as I have now come to realise.

Work was to be the place that I met Nuala Hanna. And Nuala Hanna changed my life. Initially work colleagues and then friends for a short while, we began to go out together in November 1994. By this time, the first ceasefires had been announced and a lot of the violence I had been accustomed to had stopped. It felt like a blessed time of opportunity and possibility for Northern Ireland. And it was a blessed time of opportunity for me as well, as Nuala and I became very close, very quickly. We married in November 1995.

Over the next few years, Nuala and I changed jobs several times. She moved into the field of social work, while I moved into the field of mental health, working still with children and families. And then, in 1998, we started our own family. Our eldest child, Brendan, was born eighteen days after the signing of the Good Friday Agreement. Our 'Good Friday child' brought us the same hope for the future that the Agreement brought the country. I remember at this time the relief that I had never bought into physical-force politics, or the myths of otherness that hold that tradition up. It seemed that the Agreement sought to dispel these myths of otherness. At last, I found myself living in a place where peace and prosperity were the buzzwords of our politics.

After Brendan came Joe and then Eimear, and our family was complete. A curious thing began to happen in my faith life during those years, very much related to the advent of parenthood. As my children grew, the seed of faith grew within me as well. As they prepared for their sacraments, I found myself being prepared as well – for what, I did not know. Even so, I began to move closer to the church, closer to my parish and closer to the practice of faith that was so important in my younger days. I remember it fondly and I am grateful for the enduring Spirit of God that worked so hard on me, and that has to keep working on me, mess that I am!

During that time, which I now describe as a period of conversion for me, several people were put in my path who had a great influence on me.

Kevin was a social work colleague of mine when I worked in the mental health system. He was one of only two people I knew at work who spoke openly about being people of faith. Kevin lived near me and I got to know him well enough to share with him my return to faith after the birth of my children. In particular, I shared with him that when I was attending Mass I often felt that I was about to burst into tears – not tears of sadness, but tears from a place I didn't quite understand. I was embarrassed to share this and was almost certain he wouldn't understand. We were in a car park in Downpatrick.

'Oh, right. That's the Holy Spirit,' he said, quite matter-of-fact.

'Are … are you sure? It feels really embarrassing.'

'Yep, it's the Spirit. God is telling you something.'

'What is he telling me?'

'I don't know. But I know how you might find out …' he told me with a glint in his eye.

Kevin invited me to join a local charismatic prayer group that day in the car park in Downpatrick. Who knew that the Holy Spirit would show up there?! I joined the prayer group and stayed with it for some years. It helped me deepen my prayer life and gave me a way to develop an understanding of scripture as well as ways to talk about the gospel. It was another formative time for me.

Back at my home parish, I met Father Tom Toner, who came to our parish as an older man, unwell with cancer. However, he was a tonic for us all. He preached with real energy, compassion and insight. I often sat listening to him, feeling like I was the only person in the church and that his words were only for me. We became firm friends and he encouraged me to read scripture, pray and do good works. He ministered to me in the most encouraging way. I grew in my faith under his tutelage.

And so you can imagine my sadness when Tom's cancer worsened and he got to the point where it was inevitable that he would die from the disease. Many people would have, understandably, gone into themselves, shut themselves off from others. Not Tom. He continued to minister to all his friends and parishioners, even when his public ministry had to be let go. This caused him such pain. He often told me that he ached to say public Mass again. He was every inch the priest.

Tom taught me so much about life. He also taught me so much about dying. He eventually died with great dignity, deep trust in God and love for his fellow man. This included people from other faith traditions. For Tom had an ecumenical heart. He was able to develop friendships across the apparent political and religious divides. I watched and learned at his feet. He was a good teacher and was one of the people who instilled in me a desire to reach out beyond my own community. He died in November 2013. I miss him terribly.

In the years leading up to Tom's death, my life changed radically. Owing to those in whom I had seen and heard Jesus and, of course, the hard work of the Holy Spirit, I began to sense a calling to a different life; a life closer to the Jesus I saw in others, the Jesus I was enthralled by as I read the gospels, the Jesus I had come to love deeply. But I was no longer a fourteen-year-old boy considering the priesthood. I was in my thirties, and not only that – I was married with children. I had spent so much time with people at the margins of society, with all the complications that life throws at us. I was far from 'traditional' in my views of church and religion. How could I serve the Church I grew up in as such a married lay person? But, with God's grace, and just before Tom died, that change of life happened. I was nudged out of social work and into a life in ministry. It was a kind of homecoming, alright.

REFLECTION

Alan and Jim have highlighted the following issues in this chapter:
1. The raw pain of grief and violence
2. That poverty enforces segregation and suspicion of the other
3. The unexpected nudges of the Spirit

Reflect
In what ways do you see these challenges in your own life experience?

Challenge
Having read these reflections, in what ways do you hear God challenging you to discover Jesus in the other?

Pray
John 19:25-27
Luke 4:1-2

NOTES

1. Brooks, *The Second Mountain*, p. 35.
2. Brian D. McLaren, *A Generous Orthodoxy*, Grand Rapids, MI: Zondervan, 2004, p. 70.
3. Jonathan Sacks, *Celebrating Life: Finding Happiness in Unexpected Places*, London: Bloomsbury, 2013, p. xiv.

CHAPTER FIVE

Community, Call and Ministry

ALAN > Questions and Decorating

It all happened so quickly. There were various farewells, packing, moving house (to temporary accommodation at first) and adjusting to a new environment. I was also nervous, excited, young and inexperienced. The move from being an assistant to being in charge meant entering a different world. As a curate I was forgiven many things because I was still learning and the responsibility lay elsewhere. From the moment of my institution as rector, the buck stopped with me. However, there was also growing excitement and anticipation as Liz was expecting our first child. In fact, we moved from our temporary accommodation into the rectory a few days before Peter was born.

The parish of St John Baptist, Helen's Bay, was in a beautiful location and was by and large part of Belfast's commuter belt. Houses were generally expensive and most people were financially secure. The beach was walking distance from the church and our home. Helen's Bay Presbyterian was the only other church and there were close working relations. There was also a four-church fellowship that included Glencraig Parish and Ballygilbert Presbyterian. It was a privilege to share in this group and to have a safe place to chat and pray.

My church experience to this point had shaped my thinking about ministry and parish life. There were many issues that concerned me even in these early years of ordained ministry. In general, local parishes are risk-averse; there is a dependence on one person to be and do the ministry – that is, the ordained minister. It is often a select few influential parishioners who shape the essence and direction of parish life. St John's, Helen's Bay, was no exception, and it certainly helped me realise the importance of patience in ordained ministry. I did find it challenging to be such a young rector in a parish that was not very keen on change. However, there was time to offer pastoral care and support to many people. There were the usual challenges of parish life – fundraising, maintaining old buildings and getting volunteers to help with various activities. My work with local radio kept me connected to clergy and people from across the religious divide in our community.

These years were very important to us as a family. Peter and Ruth were born while we were in this parish. The rectory was their first home. The children brought much joy into our lives, and it was also a delight for the parish to have young children in the rectory. As someone who had lost his father at a young age, it was very special being a father, and working from home gave me time to enjoy our children. We lived in a beautiful place with the beach and a coastal path within walking distance from our home. It was an amazing gift to have the normality of family life in the rarefied context of parish life.

The years in Helen's Bay were to end sooner than expected when I was appointed to St Columbanus, Ballyholme. This was a relatively new parish and my predecessor, Canon Jack Mercer, had been its first and only rector. It was a large and growing parish. There was another temporary house for us as the rectory was being renovated. Moving parish was a disorientating experience as I had to learn many more faces and names. Every parish has different customs and expectations so I had to spend time listening and grasping the nuances of every conversation.

One of the encouragements of this new context was the strong four-church friendship and collaboration. There were various shared events, including worship and clergy gatherings. I have always enjoyed the opportunity to hear about other faith journeys and traditions. It is also wonderful when we can bear witness together to the unity that is God's gift to us in Jesus. The joint Holy Week services, including a dawn service on Easter morning on the beach, were memorable.

The parish was busy, but I had the support of being part of a team ministry. This team changed and evolved in my time in the parish, but it was always an important reminder that ministry is not an individual offering. We are all called to be part of the ministry that is offered as a gift in Christ's name. In the pressured environment of parish life, it was critical to take time to listen and reflect upon what the busyness of being was doing to my interior life of faith. It was a delight to discover the Sisters of Adoration resident in a parochial house in Donaghadee, six miles from the parish of Ballyholme. This became a place of welcome, silence and hospitality. The small chapel, meeting room and a kitchen to boil a kettle were all provided with such attention to detail. The hospitality of houses of prayer is something I have come to value and need over the many years of hectic ministry. These places have been 'thin places' for me, where earth and heaven are almost touching.

One of the joys in my years in Ballyholme was being invited to speak at the charismatic prayer group that met in St Comgall's Parish Centre, Bangor. This was part of the local Roman Catholic parish and it was a thrill and pleasure to share with its members on a regular basis. They were encouraging and affirming, and I found it delightful to listen to their personal stories of faith. Their commitment to their parish, clergy and community was inspiring.

The worship was gentle and silence was an important part of discerning the 'still small voice' of God (1 Kgs 19:12). It is always people who help me discover Jesus in a different context and I was enriched and blessed by their faith and discipleship.

We had been friends for many years because of my work for Downtown Radio, but it was a delight when Father Gerry Patton was appointed parish priest of St Comgall's, a parish that also included the churches in Ballyholme and Donaghadee. The Sisters of Adoration were part of this parish grouping. On arrival, he was determined to rearrange the parochial house to create public and private spaces. There were many parishioners giving him advice on decorations and colour schemes, especially for his private quarters, but he had visited the rectory on several occasions and was impressed by Liz's choice of colours. I know I am biased, but she has always had a wonderful eye for interior decoration. Gerry asked Liz for advice and she helped him decide on the internal décor of the parochial house. He was delighted to tell others that a Protestant helped choose it!

In the early 1990s, the town of Bangor was twinned with the city of Bregenz in Austria. As part of this twinning, there were various exchange visits. Gerry and I were intrigued to receive an invitation to join some councillors from Bangor for one of these visits. We were given a brief to meet with local clergy in Bregenz and share our story of faith in the divided community of Northern Ireland. The trip was arranged and we joined the councillors for a week.

After the welcome reception, the councillors retired to their hotel, and Gerry and I were driven to our accommodation, a monastery on the outskirts of the city. It was pitch dark when we arrived at this intimidating building. The large, black, iron gates were closed, and as we opened these gates the vista was not very welcoming. It was also a school and the buildings were in darkness.

We made our way to the imposing entrance and rang a hand bell on the wall beside the door. Then we noticed, on an upper floor, the light of a candle moving down what was obviously a stairway. At this point Gerry informed me that the monks were probably a silent order. We were shown to our accommodation on the third floor by an elderly monk carrying a candle who put his finger to his lips, signalling in no uncertain terms that we were to be silent. Suffice to say, Gerry's room was much bigger. We then proceeded to ask our host, in sign language, where the toilet was. Eventually we were left on our own to try and get some sleep.

We were impressed by our surroundings, but concerned about how we were going to fulfil our duties during the following week. We needed to be transported from our accommodation in the early morning and back again late at night. This was going to be difficult without some disruption to our hosts and there was nowhere for us to recover during the very busy days. In the early hours of the morning the bell for prayers woke us and continued to do so every hour until seven o'clock. When we emerged from our rooms we discovered a frantic and confusing scene. We had missed breakfast and there were police patrolling the corridors. There had been a break-in during the night and chaos reigned.

Our host from the local council arrived to take us back to the gathering in Bregenz. We had already decided that staying in this beautiful place was inappropriate for the purpose of our trip. When we met with our travelling companions we suggested – although I think we actually insisted – that we should move into the city and stay in the hotel where they were staying. It was full, but there were two rooms in a nearby hotel. Arrangements were made and we stayed in those rooms for the rest of our visit.

One of our tasks was to meet with the clergy of Bregenz, so with the help of the local government administrative staff a meeting was organised. We met for coffee and many of the local clergy attended.

It was fascinating that it took two clergymen from across the divide in Northern Ireland to get them to meet together, as they didn't normally have much interaction. They were also fascinated to realise that Gerry and I were actually friends and worked together very well. 'There is one body and one Spirit, just as you were called to the one hope of your calling, one Lord, one faith, one baptism, one God and Father of us all, who is above all and through all and in all' (Eph 4:4-6). The image of our community divided by killings and sectarian behaviour is well known, but it is only part of the story. In Bregenz they heard a song of hope, prefiguring the hope that the Belfast Good Friday Agreement would bring.

Gerry and I enjoyed being part of this twinning exercise and were able to discuss lessons learned and experiences shared. It was a wonderful trip, but when we arrived home I drove Gerry back to his parochial house and before he got out of my car he said, 'This is when I envy you, Alan. You are going home to your family to share your experience and have a laugh together. I am going into an empty house and four walls.' That comment struck me forcefully. Ministry is a very lonely place and I could not have survived it without the love and support of my family. I do pray for those who have to endure the loneliness of ministry on their own; these disciples need our prayers. However, I also believe that celibacy is something that should not be enforced.

I am not sure how it happened, but this was a time when different chapters of my life connected. My dear friend from university, Brendan McAllister, was now leading Mediation Northern Ireland, and he had been in conversations with the RUC to help with cross-community awareness and training. Hence an invitation from Brendan for Gerry and me to be involved. It was another opportunity for us to work together.

The first of our sessions was in Garnerville at the training depot with the recruits for the RUC. After the first set of sessions, however, we were encouraged to move out of the training centre to the local area so the recruits could see the different church settings. It gave us the opportunity to explain church furnishings and practices. One of the key aspects of the training was for the recruits to experience healthy inter-church relationships, mutual understanding and respect. These were fascinating encounters and Gerry faced the more difficult questions, especially around the burial of people who had perpetrated acts of violence against their colleagues. I will not answer for Gerry, but I do know that often funerals are not just for the dead who have been baptised; they are a critical part of the excruciating journey of grief for those who are bereaved.

The signing of the Good Friday Agreement was an historic moment for this beautiful and tortured place that is my home. It was not welcomed by all as there were difficult compromises needed to get a political deal done. I believe it took courageous leaders to try and sell the unpalatable to their supporters. There was an air of hope and excitement for some, but for others there was anger and frustration.

In our divided society there are many misunderstandings and perceptions that are rooted in myth and handed down from one generation to another. It is critical that we do not accept what we have been told other people believe, but explore and discover what someone else believes in conversation with them. The division in our community has been caused by very real hurt and pain, but it is often fostered by an unwillingness to have encounters with the other. I find this sad among people who are seeking to follow Jesus and discover in him the unity that is ours as his gift. My experience of encounter has enriched, challenged and inspired me as a disciple of Jesus.

The impression that some Christians give is that they have found the perfect church and that everyone else is wrong. This kind of fundamentalism appears in different guises and in different traditions. I have been shaped and influenced by many people from many traditions other than my own. One of the key characteristics in fellow disciples that has caught my attention is that of humility. In my experience, people who have shown me the loveliness of Jesus are those who recognise they are on a journey and do not have all the answers.

Discipleship is about recognising our dependence upon God. Humility recognises that faith is not about certainty, but about trust in the God who has never given up on us. Questions are an important part of faith and discovering how others have found Jesus present with them inspires and encourages me on my journey. We are all part of God's story and, as such, our collective story as people of faith helps me on my own faith journey. This three-dimensional aspect of faith has been a blessing to me.

JIM > Angels on the Road

My mum would see me to the door for 7.10 a.m. with the words, 'Say a wee prayer for me, son. I'll have your breakfast waiting,' and I would set off. The mornings were invariably cold, wet and dark. The lack of consistent street lighting made the dark spots in between lights feel even blacker and even scarier. The walk from my house in Arizona Street to St Teresa's Church took about ten minutes. I was an altar boy and served the altar every morning during Lent. While Mass started at 7.30 a.m., I liked to be there ten minutes ahead of time to help the priest set the altar.

I'd walk down Arizona Street to the Glen Road. At the bottom of our street I'd look up and down the road to see if there was anyone about. Usually I was alone. I'd pull up the zip of my snorkel jacket so that the hood would form a kind of tunnel stretching about a foot in front of my face. This had the double benefit of keeping me warm and limiting my ability to see what was around me in the almost impenetrable darkness.

With a cold shiver in my bones and a nervous chatter in my teeth, off I'd go, praying that I'd reach the church safely and not be 'got' by anyone or anything in the darkness. The quiet and the darkness magnified my sense of loneliness in those walks. And in the loneliness, my boy's mind played all sorts of tricks. Every branch waving in the wind became a sinister arm with a hand at the end pointing bony fingers at me. Each dog barking became a wild werewolf baying for my blood. And if I saw someone coming towards me? Well, that petrified me the most. Who were they? What would they do? Surely they were a serial killer out to snare a victim? We had plenty of crazed killers roaming the dark streets of Belfast in 1983.

There was only one person who could approach me on those cold mornings and bring a sense of calm. The father of my friend Denis Kearney, himself also called Denis – but always Mr Kearney to me – worked night shifts in the local brewery, and when he was working he finished just in time to be walking home at the same time that I was going to serve Mass. It got that I could recognise his figure through my snorkel hood from quite a distance. Seeing him on those cold, scary walks brought me great relief. I knew I would be safe when I saw Mr Kearney coming. I focused on him to the exclusion of the imaginary pointing fingers, werewolves and serial killers. When we met he would give me a big smile – his face lit up – and, knowing I was going to Mass, say something like, 'Say one for me, Jim.' 'I will,' I'd answer and move on with a bit of a skip in my step, buoyed up with the confidence gained by meeting a friendly face on the dark street. I'd serve the altar and emerge into the relief of daytime light on the Glen Road.

God rest his soul, Mr Kearney is dead now. He lived and died a family man, and a good one at that. He was an angel to me on those mornings. He probably didn't know the reassurance he brought to me, but it certainly made an impact. Like all angels, he carried with him a message. His was that all was well and that I was on the right path. And how I have needed angels in my life, reassuring me that all is well and that I am on the right path.

By 2009, I had been in social work for sixteen years and it had been good to me. Nuala and I were able to buy our house and build a home with, and for, our children. We were able to take family holidays during the summer to our beloved Algarve town of Lagos. Both of us had moved into management, along with which came responsibility and challenge. Nuala is a remarkable woman. She is quiet and unassuming, introverted by nature, and yet she is a tremendously strong leader. She brings clarity and guidance for others in the most difficult of situations – families in crisis, placement breakdowns for fostered and adopted children, child protection crises. She has been in the right job all of her career, and her talents have been noticed along the way. She has moved into senior leadership in the health service and I am very proud – in awe, even – of her.

Back in 2009 I was managing several teams of social workers across different settings, and yet I had the feeling that, unlike Nuala, I wasn't in the right job; I wasn't on the right path. It was a feeling that I had wrestled with for quite some time before that. It coincided with my getting more involved in my parish life, taking on duties as a Minister of the Word and of Holy Communion, as well as getting involved in fundraising and other important parish initiatives.

I found real solace and consolation in prayer. I read the scriptures, searching for and finding verses and stories that seemed to speak directly to my situation. In particular, 2 Corinthians 4:8-11 became an important 'go to' piece of scripture:

> We are afflicted in every way, but not crushed; perplexed, but not driven to despair; persecuted, but not forsaken; struck

down, but not destroyed; always carrying in the body the death of Jesus, so that the life of Jesus may also be made visible in our bodies. For while we live, we are always being given up to death for Jesus' sake, so that the life of Jesus may be made visible in our mortal flesh.

It helped me remember that trials are part of life, and even more a part of spiritual life. And it consoled me to know that, even through the greatest of trials, we are never truly beaten – God is with us. And so I leaned more and more on God.

I remember being based for a year or so in a children's home in North Belfast. A hundred yards up the road was the local Catholic parish church. On my breaks I would go to the church and sit in the silence and warmth of the building, praying – sometimes with words, mostly in silent listening. When my watch reminded me that my break time was up, I always felt a huge wrench leaving the church. It struck me that I was existing in two houses – the children's home and the house of God. Not only that, but I felt a stronger draw to the house of God than I did to the children's home, great and all as the people and the work there were. I felt at a crossroads and I wasn't sure what to do. And then the angels arrived …

Two women came to visit, one out of the blue and one invited. Both were angels of a kind, with messages for me. The first was a long-term friend of mine who was going through family turmoil. She came to see me one day, unannounced and in a state of despair. As soon as she came into the room where I was, she fell into my arms crying. All I could do was hold her and absorb her sobs. We stood like that for a long time. Eventually, she asked me, 'Does God love me?' It was a question from the heart. It was a question she truly did not know the answer to. It was a question we all ask at some time or other. And it was a question that *I* knew the answer to. I replied that God did love her and, indeed, that she was the apple of God's eye. Not a religious person, then or now, but a person with the most incredible spirituality, kindness, wisdom and sense of selfless service to others, my friend took my words of reassurance as truth and the tears stopped, allowing us to talk through the crisis she was facing.

What a gift this angel gave me that day. She told me, without needing to tell me, that I had a role in life bringing God's love to light. In that moment, something shifted inside me, letting me know that this act of service was integral to how I would live my life from now on. It reminded me of the scripture passage from Hebrews that tells us to show hospitality even to strangers, because we can often entertain angels without knowing it. Isn't it so true? Angels come to us in all sorts of ways. Under all sorts of guises. But they always bring a message or an insight.

My second angel came to me invited and with the express purpose of helping me find my path. Late in 2009, I knew that I had a decision to make about my future. The draw to the house of God, to prayer, to a life lived more overtly orientated to sharing God's love, was almost overwhelming. I reached out to Caren, a lifelong friend, who I knew had a job working in a retreat centre for young people. I admired her commitment to working for God. I wanted to share with her my own feelings and get a sense of what I could do about them.

Caren is a generous person and she spent a lot of time listening to me and advising me in relation to what to pray for; where to look for possible avenues for work. She cautioned me that moving from social work would bring with it a drop in wages and a change in working hours. She was realistic, sensible and wise. I left our meeting with a clearer sense that I was being called to something else in my life and with a sense of consolation that if I kept myself open to the God of all possibilities, something would turn up in my life to put me on the right path.

For some, God turns up in burning bushes, with drama and fanfare. Not so for me. Looking back at my life, I see how God turns up unexpectedly, quietly, gently and when least expected, mostly in the form of other people. In December 2009, God turned up with a gentle tap on the shoulder as I was leaving Mass on a dark and cold Saturday night.

'Jim, you have experience doing group work, don't you?' It was my parish priest.

'I do.'

'The diocese is looking for people to do some voluntary group work as part of a listening exercise the bishop wants to conduct. Would you like to be part of the team?'

And there it was. With this gentle tap on the shoulder, the invitation to get involved, my life changed.

'Yes, I'd like that very much. Thank you.'

'Good man. I'll be in touch with times and dates.'

True to his word, my parish priest came back to me and gave me the details I needed to get to the first meeting of what would become the 'Listening Process' in the Diocese of Down and Connor. After a couple of months' training, I was sent out with another person to several parishes around our diocese to listen to the people and their desires for the Church going forward. It was an electrifying experience. As I travelled across the diocese, I felt like I was on a mission. Gathering with people, praying in community with them and discerning where God was pulling us felt to me, at last, like the right path for me to take.

The listening concluded at Easter 2011 and I was invited to be part of a small team charged with producing a report on what was heard. Also on that team were Paula McKeown, Father Alan McGuckian SJ (now Bishop of Raphoe) and Father Martin Magill. These three, as we will see in time, were to play a big part in my life story from now on.

One of the key themes that came out of the listening we conducted, and that found its way into our report, was the need for increased lay participation in the Catholic Church. In a way, this theme encapsulated the journey I had been on. The perception was, and still is for many, that unless you were ordained – and therefore a man and celibate – avenues to serious involvement were not open to you. Now, that is an over-simplification and not entirely true, and yet there was, and still is, some truth in that perception. We were challenged then to begin to rethink how leadership can be exercised within a very hierarchically structured church system. It is a journey, and we are not near the destination yet, although I believe we are making progress.

Increased Lay Participation was one of five key themes that emerged from our report (with Open and Welcoming Community, Passing on the Faith, Faith and Worship, and Care of the Clergy being the other four). In order to begin to implement some action based on the report, Paula, Alan and I began to do some very basic parish development work in a few parishes, bearing in mind that all three of us had full-time jobs – Paula and I in the health service, Alan as a member of the Jesuit community in Belfast.

I remember one conversation in particular around that time. Alan and I had been to Portaferry to work with the parish pastoral council there. We had had a very encouraging evening and on the way back in the car Alan said, 'I want to ask you a question and I want you to think about it before answering.'

How very Ignatian, I thought.

'Sure. Fire away.'

'How would you feel if you never did any more of this work we are doing together?'

The question hit me in the chest. It took the breath from me, really unexpectedly.

I sat with it for a while and could only reply with one word.

'Sad,' I said.

Alan didn't speak. He closed his eyes and nodded. I got the impression he was praying and so I said nothing, but prayed silently for most of the journey home.

That night saw a final shift take place within me. As I look back now I can see it. God had gently and slowly brought me through a process of being able to let go of one life and look forward to another. As I said the word 'sad' in the car with Alan, I knew with certainty that I would be following a new path from then on. It would be a path where I would share God's love, share the scriptures and work with the people of God, wherever I had something to offer. Even though I didn't know how I was to do this, I had the certainty and the conviction that I would do it somehow. My years of anxious searching were over. My searching would continue – it always has, in some ways – but the anxiety about the search faded away.

The car speeding back to Belfast was taking me towards a career change, with a move into pastoral ministry. Some six months after that night in Portaferry, the diocese established the Living Church Office and charged it with rolling out the actions associated with the Listening Process. In May 2012, I applied for and got a full-time post in the office as parish development officer (the first of three posts I would hold over the next decade). With all of this would come the joys and the dilemmas facing lay people working in the Catholic Church.

REFLECTION

Alan and Jim have highlighted the following issues in this chapter:
1. Discipleship is not just individualistic, but community-based
2. God's call is for all
3. The tension between celibacy and ordained ministry

Reflect
In what ways do you see these challenges in your own life experience?

Challenge
Having read these reflections, in what ways do you hear God challenging you to discover Jesus in the other?

Pray
Luke 10:1-8
John 13:34-35

CHAPTER SIX

Identity, Change and Discernment

ALAN > Everything Changes

My next chapter of ministry began with a life-changing phone call. Liz and I had just returned from a post-Easter break in Glasgow. Our children, Peter and Ruth, were students in Glasgow and we decided it was a great place to celebrate my fiftieth birthday. We arrived on the Sunday evening after Easter and normal parish life resumed for me on the Monday. However, on the Tuesday I returned home from our staff meeting, had a light lunch and was preparing to visit some parishioners in the Ulster Hospital, Dundonald, when the phone rang.

The role of electing a new bishop of Connor had passed to the House of Bishops, as the Electoral College had not been able to elect an agreed candidate. I had not been a candidate nor had I been asked to consider this new calling. However, the phone call to Ballyholme rectory that Tuesday lunchtime was to inform me that 'it felt good to them and the Holy Spirit to appoint me Bishop of Connor'. This was a seismic moment in life and ministry. I was in shock for days, facing the trauma of leaving a loving and supportive community, uprooting my family from their home into a new world, as yet unknown. However, I was certain that one of my aims would be to live in the unity that God gives us in Jesus.

This unity is something that is always under threat from interpretations and disagreements that damage our message of grace. As Eugene Peterson wrote in his journal, 'How the so-called Christian community can generate so much hate is appalling. Haven't we learned anything about civil discourse? Will we ever? And it is so debilitating – we have this glorious gospel to proclaim and give away and we gang up against one another and throw dogma rocks.'[1] In these scribblings my focus has been on the unity across the deep divide in the community I call home, but it is important to note that, both within denominations and among all denominations, there is the danger of building disagreement into what essentially becomes schism.

The counsel of scripture, as I read it, focuses on the imperative that God has given unity as a gift; our calling is to enter into this and live it out. It is all too easy to focus on differences and disagreements that derive from our own interpretations while failing to see the validity of other interpretations. We need to learn to live agreeably with disagreement. The teaching of Jesus on the unity of the Church has to be taken very seriously in the midst of our differences.

It was eight weeks after that phone call that we left Ballyholme. The kindness, affirmation and love of the parishioners there were special gifts as we said our goodbyes. Our new home was the other side of Belfast Lough. My family were amazing in their support and encouragement, as well as enabling me to laugh at myself. I had a week to help unpack and then five days on retreat in Holy Cross Abbey in Rostrevor.

There are many aspects of spirituality that I have benefited from, thanks to my continuing friendship across the religious divide in our community. Retreats and spiritual direction helped me in the face of the constant demands of parish ministry, and helped me again as I prepared to take up my role as bishop.

When I first met the Benedictine brothers who established the Holy Cross Abbey in Rostrevor, they were living in the missionary convent there and I was the parish minister at Ballyholme. The dedication of the church and the opening of the monastery took place in 2004. It became a special place of retreat for me, where I could be refreshed and renewed by the silence, hospitality and prayer of this 'thin place'. This was the place I chose for a retreat as I prepared to enter into my new calling as a bishop.

My stay in Rostrevor was a blessing. I was given the gifts of time, prayer, and space to listen, speak and be enfolded in community prayer and hospitality. The daily rhythm of prayers in the chapel, the silent meals, and the opportunity to discuss my inner life in a safe space were invaluable. The holy space given to me by Brother Mark helped me find peace and encouragement for the journey ahead. He gave me a phrase, inspired by the Holy Spirit, that has sustained me ever since: 'holy indifference'. I was to remain indifferent to the way people treated me differently as a bishop. As a bishop, I had an important office or role, but that did not make me special or better than anyone else. My worth was in being a child of God, cherished and valued by the name in which I was baptised, Father, Son and Holy Spirit.

After the oasis of this retreat it was back to unpacking and adjusting to a new home. From the moment of my appointment I found the experience bewildering and exhausting. I found myself experiencing a wide range of emotions: joy, excitement, fear and apprehension. As I reflect on the scriptures, it strikes me that those whom God call often feel a deep reluctance and a sense of unworthiness. This has helped me over many years as I have struggled with my calling to ordained life. I have always felt inadequate, unworthy and reluctant, but have also known a peace that has been a gift from God.

The service of ordination was a special moment of encouragement and I do believe in the grace of ordination. St

Anne's Cathedral in Belfast was a holy space for the service and it was a personal privilege to be ordained in the city where I grew up. It was wonderful to have so many family members, friends and fellow disciples join in that celebration. It was a joy to have the Benedictine brothers sing during the service and to have three Roman Catholic bishops present: Bishop Paddy Walsh, Bishop Tony Farquhar and Bishop Dónal McKeown. I had met Bishop Dónal many years before and appeared with him live on radio the day the Good Friday Agreement was signed on 10 April 1998. We were guests on the Radio 5 Live morning show from a coffee shop in Belfast city centre. The host was Peter Allen, a very accomplished and experienced broadcaster. I remember him commenting on how Dónal and I were friends even though we came from different sides of this divided community. It was not surprising to us, but it reminded us of how the work of peace was still a road to be travelled.

On reflection, I found the encouragement and affirmation of my fellow disciples from across the divide an inspiration as I set out on the path of being a bishop. Central to this calling, as I saw it, was being a figure of unity within my own tradition, but also across the divisions in church and community.

This new chapter in ministry brought new experiences, new opportunities and meetings with many new people. The variety was immense and the diary had to be managed much more carefully than before. I had a tendency to want to say yes to any request and I quickly discovered that that was not sustainable. There were also complex and difficult situations that demanded my time and energy. These proved time-consuming, especially when I had no power and little ability to affect them. However, one of my priorities was any opportunity to develop relations with other church leaders.

On the first anniversary of my ordination as bishop, St Peter's Day 2008, I attended the ordination of Bishop Noël Treanor, who was the successor to Bishop Paddy Walsh as Bishop of Down and Connor. This was a wonderful celebration in St Peter's Catholic Cathedral. To share in this new chapter for Bishop Noël was an honour, and our friendship was to develop and be a great blessing in future years.

As I entered my second year as a bishop, I was thrilled to be able to attend the Lambeth Conference in Canterbury during July and August 2008. This was the fourteenth Lambeth Conference of Anglican bishops from across the globe, at the invitation of the Archbishop of Canterbury, Rowan Williams. The theme was 'bishops as leaders in mission'. The controversy surrounding the conference over the issue of same-sex relationships meant that many bishops did not attend. However, I found the experience enriching, challenging and formative as a new bishop.

The programme was intense, beginning each day with a small-group Bible study of ten to twelve bishops. This was followed by 'indaba' groups of forty bishops, and there were sixteen such groups. The idea of 'indaba' comes from South Africa and it represents an informal discussion about serious matters of concern. One of the principles to be honoured in the group discussions was that of listening to other voices and viewpoints. In the afternoons there was a wide range of seminars and gatherings. In the evenings there were plenaries with various speakers. There were two memorable evenings for me, those with Rabbi Jonathan Sacks and Brian McLaren, who were inspirational and wise. Each day was enfolded in gatherings for prayer, Eucharist and meals. It was not a restful experience, but it was enriching.

When our 'indaba' group met for the first time we had to appoint a listener, someone who would record the discussion and bring it back to the group the next day for approval. I was appointed our group listener. There were sixteen listeners and our job during the three-week conference was to write up a final document. We met every day after our group sessions to record our individual group reflections and attempt to merge these into one document, entitled 'Capturing Conversations and Reflections from the Lambeth Conference 2008'. It was an extraordinary task – and exhausting. However, it gave me insights into the nuances of the fascinating discussions that took place in the conference. Archbishop Rowan presented the final report on the final day of the gathering.

We discussed many subjects, including mission and evangelism, human and social justice, environment, ecumenism, relations with other world religions, Anglican bishops and Anglican identity, and human sexuality and scripture. There were some very robust discussions made easier by the smaller groups that had enabled friendships and relationships to grow. There was a diverse range of opinions, some of them expressed very forcefully. The liberal and conservative voices clashed, but it was a safe place. Only one day was set aside for the topic of same-sex attraction and relationships, but there was no resolution to this intractable issue.

There were important lessons for me drawn from a very involved commitment to the conference. My mind was not changed on the critical importance of Jesus' teaching on the unity of the Church. I still find it difficult to declare someone else no longer a member of the Church over matters where there is serious disagreement between people of deep faith in Jesus. The truth that people can argue for is cancelled out by the anger and stridency of their voices. This applies to people on both sides of disagreements I have witnessed, whether on a global scale or in local churches.

One of the funny moments of Lambeth happened on the day we were discussing ecumenism. I had been asked to speak in our 'indaba' about ecumenical relationships in Northern Ireland. There was shock and disbelief from some of our group when I described the friendships I enjoyed with my local Roman Catholic clergy when I was in parish life and with the Roman Catholic bishops

I now served with in Connor. The expectation expressed by some of the group, based on the images they had seen in the news, was of a very fractured community divided between Roman Catholics and Protestants. However, it is the case that many people from both sides of the community have worked hard at building mutual understanding and peaceful relations.

After our group meeting some of us went together to one of the dining rooms for lunch. The first person we met as we entered the room was the Vatican observer for that day, Bishop Tony Farquhar. I was able to introduce him to some members of our group and we dined together, helping them witness the friendship that I had talked about in the morning session. The fact that Bishop Tony greeted me with a hug helped my case as well!

This Lambeth experience of living with different viewpoints undoubtedly helped shape my years as a bishop. The lessons learned left an indelible mark on my thinking; the critical importance of listening and the recognition of other perspectives; and the vital need to live the unity of the Church that God has declared in Jesus. I returned home exhausted, but inspired and encouraged.

During the next number of years my friendship with Bishop Noël Treanor continued to grow and we determined to do what we could together. On Saturday, 7 March 2009, there was a terrible attack on the Massereene army barracks in Antrim. Two young soldiers were murdered and four others, including two pizza delivery men, were injured in the attack. The two soldiers killed were about to leave Northern Ireland for a tour of Afghanistan. They were Mark Quinsey, twenty-three, from Birmingham and Cengiz 'Patrick' Azimkar, twenty-one, from Wood Green, London.

On the Monday after this terrible atrocity, Bishop Noël and I visited two civilians injured in the shooting, who were being treated in Antrim Area Hospital. We spoke with them and their families and prayed with them. As we listened to the hospital staff and the people we met, we were reminded of the resilience in this community and the desire not to go back to the horror of violence and murder. We believed that doing this together was an important way for us to reflect our unity and our desire to build a shared future of respect and hope.

I was invited by Bishop Noël to attend the first edition of Catholic Social Days for Europe, organised by COMECE (the Commission of the Bishops' Conferences of the European Community). This event, held in Gdansk, Poland, 8–11 October 2009, was an ambitious attempt to engage Catholics from across Europe in an examination of the economic, social, political and cultural challenges we face in all countries of Europe, informed by the social teaching of the Catholic Church.

I was an ecumenical visitor and greatly enjoyed the hospitality and the excellent presentations and discussions. I also revelled in the shared craic of being in a group of people from Ireland. The insights from different perspectives, voices and locations were refreshing and challenging.

When I had been serving as bishop for three years I found myself in hospital for emergency surgery to remove my gall bladder. However, as I prepared to return to work, it became clear that I was emotionally exhausted or burnt out. I had to take further time off and I was prescribed anti-depressants. To be diagnosed with a mental health problem was disturbing and confusing. I was suffering from depression and I found this very uncomfortable. The personal learning from this has been helpful, but difficult. I received wonderful help from cognitive therapy. I discovered that I was trying to fix things that I could not and taking responsibility for issues that I should not. Much of this stems from my experience in childhood and I am very grateful for the professional help I received from my GP and therapist.

In the months that it took to recover sufficiently to allow me to return to work, it was wonderful to receive so many messages from fellow disciples. I was very encouraged and blessed by the many Mass cards I received as people promised to pray for me. The prayers of the Church are so important as we journey with Jesus; they carry us when we need to be carried and help us to know and experience the presence of Jesus with us. In discovering Jesus in the other, I have learned so much about the 'body of Christ' here on earth. Many fellow disciples seek to be part of what they call the 'true' Church, holding dearly to dogma and denominations. Increasingly, I have found the gift of unity present in people when I have been willing to search for and discover Jesus in them, rather than judging them by what they say or believe or by what denomination they belong to.

> You cannot deal with a perfect, all-loving, all-forgiving, all-understanding God in heaven, if you cannot deal with a less-than-perfect, less-than-forgiving, and less-than-understanding community here on earth. You cannot pretend to be dealing with an invisible God if you refuse to deal with a visible family.[2]

JIM > Identity

Belfast, 1981. The slap stung my face. It brought tears to my eyes; not crying, as such, but a bodily reaction to the shock of the attack. The sting of the word that followed was worse:

'Traitor!'

My house growing up was in a street built in several stages. The first stage, from the first half of the twentieth century, had been built by a Belfast man 'done well'. He had moved to Arizona in the southwest of the USA and had made some money. He returned to his home town and decided to build some houses a couple of miles outside the centre of Belfast. Appropriately, he named the street after his promised land of opportunity and wealth: Arizona Street. These first few houses were (and still are) quite grand. One or two were three-storey. Others were two-storey but substantial.

In the early years of the street's development it housed mainly Protestant people, who came to the area to work on the farms that would have occupied the land at that time. The 1920s was a troubled time and, like other streets in other areas, our street went through a period of upheaval, with its residents being forced to move out due to the threat of violence. Consequently, the street and the area around it saw the arrival of more Catholic people than Protestant people as the years went on.

On into the 1950s and beyond, the street grew in size – although the houses did the opposite. Arizona Street became a street of terraced houses topped and tailed by the bigger houses built earlier in the century at one end and a row of what had been labourers' cottages at the other. It was a cul-de-sac and, as cul-de-sacs are wont to do, it became a little enclosed community of families and friends. No through traffic (either automotive or footfall) disrupted street life. And that was good.

By the time I was growing up there, the area was clearly identified with the Catholic, nationalist, republican community. Indeed, our past as having once been a thriving Protestant community had been all but lost to the mists of time. If you'd asked any of those living there, they'd probably have told you that the area had always been as it was then. Identity is a bit like that. We experience it in the present and make assumptions that it has always been thus. However, our history is always more complex and more fluid than the rigidity of our story of the present. Yes, we were fairly certain in our identity back then.

Another important feature of life when I was growing up in the 1970s and 1980s was the proximity of our street to Milltown Cemetery. That, in turn, meant that our street was very close to the political demonstrations and high-profile funerals that regularly took place during that time. These events were well-attended and noisy affairs. From our vantage point in Arizona Street we could see the people filing down the Glen Road to demonstrations and then hear the noise of the crowd as it cheered whatever speaker happened to be orating on that occasion.

As time went on, and as the violence of the Troubles wreaked havoc for all in its path, these demonstrations drew increasing attention from the security services, and this meant an abundance of British soldiers around the streets surrounding Milltown Cemetery. A handy spot for the army to park up (just far enough away from Milltown so as not to be in the middle of a hostile crowd and close enough to get to that crowd if ordered) was the bottom of my street. And so it was a common sight to see a Saracen (which we saw as a kind of army jeep when we were young; it's only now as an adult that I realise that a Saracen is actually a heavily armoured personnel carrier – basically, a tank without the tracks) or three, sitting at the bottom of the street with soldiers standing around talking, waiting on orders. Usually these soldiers were there for a short time and then moved on.

We played football at the bottom of our street too. We had our 'pitch' marked out. One of our friends lived in one of the three-storey houses and the house had a garage with a small driveway attached. The gates to their driveway acted as one of our nets. The other net was a gap between two houses. Perfect! On one particular day in 1981, when I was ten years old, our football match and a political demo coincided, and so, as we played, we were watched by a group of squaddies standing around their vehicles. Time went by and the soldiers must have got bored. They watched us playing football and when the ball went close to them they kicked it back. One squaddie in particular seemed very interested in our game. He was a black soldier – one of the only black faces I'd seen in my short life. He came over and began to play football with us. He gave his rifle to one of his friends and just joined in. It was a kind of surreal experience for us. We didn't have much personal contact with soldiers and I was, for the most part, afraid of them. But this guy seemed nice. And he could play football. 'What's the harm?' I thought. So we played football for a while. And when the game reached a bit of a lull, the soldier went back to his friend and took his gun once more. But he returned to our little group of wannabe footballers and offered to let us look through the sights of his gun. I gladly accepted the offer, from what now seemed to be more of a real person than a soldier per se. I remember the feel of the gun and the sights. The gun was very heavy and the metal parts were very cold.

After a minute, the soldier wandered the few short yards away and rejoined the other squaddies. And that is when it happened. Seemingly out of nowhere, an older boy (late teens) approached me and slapped me hard in the face.

'Traitor!' He spat the word at me.

He was incensed that I had spent time with what was, to him, no doubt, the enemy; not one of 'us', someone outside of our very fixed identity. As quickly as he had appeared, the boy left. My friends looked on in silence. I was humiliated. I was ashamed. I was sore. I was afraid and confused. What was happening in our wee street? For so long it had been a haven of safety, but now the war that we heard about seemed to be coming closer to home. Never again did I look through the sights of a soldier's gun – although we were often offered this by soldiers. Never again did I play football with a soldier. As I grew up, I had several run-ins with soldiers who were not friendly like the man who played football with us that day. I was, on occasion, bullied, hit and harassed by soldiers. I saw the war in this land escalate and, as we know, many people lost their lives. Soldiers did the losing as well as the taking of life here. And every life lost and taken was a tragedy.

I still know the boy who hit me. I know a little of his story. He had his reasons to hate the British army. I would not join him in that hatred, but I can understand it, as I can understand more now why people become soldiers.

In many ways, we grew up here very quickly from children to adults. War does that. My transition from childhood innocence began that day at the bottom of Arizona Street. It was then that I realised that something very complicated and very frightening was happening in the place where I lived. I knew from that day that there were rules about who I could and could not talk to. I got to know that there were places I could and could not go – even in my own city. As I grew, I saw that the conflict here was a horror. I never bought into physical-force politics; all I saw were human beings being killed, and it pained me. And it drew me from that young age into questioning what it means to have the identity ascribed to people in my neighbourhood. It left me with a deep questioning about identity in general, and my own in particular.

I think I carry this questioning with me still. I can see now, as I look back on my first years working in ministry, that the issue of my identity was a key question for me. Having settled into my new way of life, and having left social work behind, I was really enjoying the space that God had manoeuvred me into. I got to travel all over the eastern side of Northern Ireland, the territory covered by the diocese I worked for, meeting good people everywhere. So many were trying to do their best to live lives according to the gospel and according to what the Catholic Church taught them. I am always inspired by the goodness in people. Such selflessness, generosity of spirit and encouragement can only come from God.

The job I was in also manoeuvred me into the position of leading people in prayer and the discernment of God's will. In the Catholic tradition, this is a fairly unusual role for a lay person to hold in terms of an official position. I embraced the role and, thank God, was competent enough in it for people to have a good experience.

It did, however, bring up the question of identity for me once more; not only for me, but for others I spoke to as well. By 2015, I had felt a stirring for some time, somewhere deep within me, to explore the possibility of becoming ordained as a permanent deacon. A permanent deacon is a man (in the Catholic tradition, only men can be ordained into holy orders) who is ordained into three areas of ministry: the Altar, the Word, and Charity. He serves the altar when the priest celebrates Mass. He can proclaim the gospel and preach the sermon afterwards. And he always commits to serving the poor, the vulnerable, the ill, and the disadvantaged.

Many people had said to me through the years that they thought I was right for that vocation. I, too, felt that I was right for this vocation, and so I applied to my diocese when the diaconate was introduced. I was accepted onto the programme and began what is called a propaedeutic year or a year of discernment. The year was punctuated with weekends away on retreat and reflection, spiritual direction and plenty of personal prayer.

I found the experience very rewarding indeed. However, part way through the year I began to experience some movements within me away from the idea that this was the right path. I recognise this much more in hindsight than I did at the time. Back then, I think I ignored or even denied these feelings. There was something about the adoption of this identity as an ordained person that I felt would give me a sense of certainty and – again, in hindsight, I have the words I didn't have at the time – I think I felt it would in some way validate the work I was doing and the calling I had received to minister to people.

I 'doubled down' and threw myself into visualising myself as a deacon. I allowed the comments of others who sought to encourage me to become more important or more persuasive than they should have been. I read and reread articles and books about the diaconate.

I was overdoing things. I was not praying in freedom, seeking what God wanted; I was praying to confirm that what I wanted was good. As the year progressed, I got tired. I often find that. When I am out of tune with what God is calling me to, my body gets tired. And so it went.

As the year continued, though, and as I got more and more tired, I began to bring my experience to my spiritual director, who helped me to get back in tune with God by praying more honestly and being more open to listening to what God was telling me.

It's funny how God moves. I had a moment of clarity that helped me in my discernment. It's funny because it happened in the shower, of all places. I remember one day having a sense of God saying to me, 'You are a lay person and a lay person you will remain. It is as a lay person that you will do my work.' I didn't hear a voice from above, of course, but I clearly heard that sentence resound within me. And with it came a sense of peace, calm and consolation that I had not felt for many months. All of a sudden everything became clear. The previous months I had been in a state of desolation, experiencing tiredness and concern, and yet I had been blinded to the lessons that desolation could have taught me. I resolved in the shower that morning to submit a letter asking to leave the diaconate programme. Thank God, many others continued with the programme and were ordained at the end of it. The ministry of the deacon itself is a good thing – just not my thing.

Holding on to our perceived notions of identity can do us harm. We've seen it here in Northern Ireland when we have allowed identity to trump compassion, friendship and forgiveness. It has led to great hurt for us all. And in the spiritual life, holding too tightly to a perceived 'right' identity, to the exclusion of God's call, can also do harm. I see now, with the benefit of some years of hindsight, that my experience of exploring the diaconal path, as well as being one of great learning, cost me a lot in terms of stress, worry and overworking to the point of burnout. And it came from a place of feeling that identity had value over the call. We face a major challenge in all churches to really understand the call of God to our people. Perhaps, in the very cleric-centred world of Catholicism, we have an even bigger challenge. Lay people can and are called by God to exercise all sorts of charisms for the good of the Church and the good of the world. Do our structures allow for the embracing of these charisms? Or do they sometimes lead to a privileging of some over others? I ask these questions as what is called in Irish *cara criticiúil*, a critical friend. Until we see Jesus and his giftedness in all of our people, we might just be missing God's call to the Church.

Thank God, I have continued to live into God's call to minister as a lay person. And God has continued to put good people in my path to minister to me on that journey. Indeed, God was to soon take me on a new path, one that invited me to a deep encounter with people from other Christian traditions.

REFLECTION

Alan and Jim have highlighted the following issues in this chapter:
1. The danger of investing importance in assumed difference
2. Our identity in Christ
3. The ongoing tension between ordained and lay ministries

Reflect
In what ways do you see these challenges in your own life experience?

Challenge
Having read these reflections, in what ways do you hear God challenging you to discover Jesus in the other?

Pray
Matthew 16:13-17
Mark 10:36-38

NOTES

1. Winn Collier, *A Burning in My Bones: The Authorized Biography of Eugene Peterson, Translator of the Message*, Milton Keynes: Authentic, 2020, p. 278.

2. Ronald Rolheiser, *The Holy Longing: The Search for a Christian Spirituality* (15th anniversary ed.), New York: Image, p. 98.

CHAPTER SEVEN

Tradition, Separation and Communion

ALAN > A Wider Vision

It had been planned for two years and the timing was perfect. I
returned to work in time for a diocesan pilgrimage to the Holy
Land. Liz and I joined the large party made up of small groups from
various parishes across the diocese. The eighty-five-strong group
arrived in Tel Aviv at 9.00 p.m. on Tuesday, 22 March 2011, via
Heathrow. We were based in Jerusalem and Galilee. The pilgrimage
began in Jerusalem, where our hotel overlooked the Old City and
was within walking distance of the Holy Sepulchre. In Tiberias we
stayed in a hotel by the lake.

As well as seeing the sights in Jerusalem, we visited Bethlehem,
Nazareth, Capernaum, the Dead Sea (which, of course, is actually a
lake) and Qumran. There was a boat trip on the lake. This was the
one place that had not changed since Jesus walked these shores and
it was a holy moment for me. I then celebrated the Eucharist, for the
first time in months, on the shore of the lake. That was the moment
when I was back at work, surrounded by the love and support of
people from the diocese.

Over the years this simple and yet profound meal has become
a special encounter with Jesus and fellow disciples. Whether as a
parish priest or a bishop, it is difficult to describe the amazing joy

it is to celebrate the Eucharist with God's people. This is a mystery beyond words, and a moment of encounter for the individual and the community, as Jesus is present with us in the mess of our lives. I find Eugene Peterson's reflection on the Eucharist inspiring: 'The Eucharist puts Jesus in his place: dying on the cross and giving us that sacrificed life. And it puts us in our place: opening our hands and receiving the remission of our sins, which is our salvation.'[1]

However, this moment of communion and celebration has become a sign of our division – a moment of pain among fellow disciples. There have been theological arguments about what happens at this meal, and a meal that should unite can become a reminder of the Church's division. This is a sadness I can testify to and yet it has not damaged my relationship with fellow disciples with whom I cannot share this meal. The Spirit breathes life into the dynamic of relationship. However, Church rules and regulations can cause hurt even when they are well intentioned.

Over my years in ordained life the quiet, hospitality and spirituality of Holy Cross Abbey in Rostrevor have made it a sacred place for recovery and rest. The rhythm of prayer, sleep and good food is an oasis amid the demands and weariness of the ministry of service. However, when I stay there I am reminded of the pain of our division because I do not receive the sacrament.

In our various theological debates and disagreements, the Eucharist is a constant reminder of mystery. I cannot fully comprehend what happens when fellow disciples celebrate this meal together. God takes the ordinary and everyday and makes them special. The bread and wine become to me the body and blood of Christ. My response, to receive with open hands and heart, makes me a channel of this amazing grace. I have found the word 'mystery' helpful when I meditate upon the Eucharist. In the words of Jean-Pierre de Caussade:

'Take for example what happens in the Eucharist! And yet it remains the mystery of all mysteries in which all is so secret, unseen and incomprehensible that the more spiritual and enlightened we are, the more faith we need to believe.'[2]

I was privileged to receive an invitation to be present at and participate in the Living Church Congress. Bishop Noël Treanor invited eighteen hundred people from across the Diocese of Down and Connor to the Waterfront Hall in Belfast on Saturday, 28 September 2013. It was a privilege to be there and to take part.

Preparation for the event and the launch of a pastoral plan for the diocese involved listening to and consulting with up to three thousand people – clergy and religious in parishes, universities and groups of all kinds. The result was a co-ordinated parish plan that allowed space to set priorities that remain faithful to the spirit, locality and life of each parish. As Bishop Noël stated in his opening address, the aim of the event was 'to build a culture of creative co-responsibility in our parishes and in our diocese.'

This was a very exciting project and it was fascinating to be part of the launch. On a practical level, each parish was to establish a parish council and a finance committee. Ministries and assistant ministries were established to support the dwindling number of parish priests. What struck me very forcibly is that we in the diocese were facing very similar problems, especially across the city of Belfast.

I was asked to speak at a workshop on the subject of reconciliation and I was joined by our diocesan development officer, Trevor Douglas. My story of growing up in a fractured city and watching my local Catholic church be desecrated resonated with many of those present. Trevor told of his experience of growing up in the town of Lurgan and the scars it bore from the Troubles. This was a wonderful opportunity to share my story and also the first time I got the chance to work with Jim Deeds. His is a friendship that has brought me much blessing and learning on my journey with Jesus. He is a brother in Christ.

In October of the same year, 2013, I found myself in Busan, South Korea. I was the Church of Ireland representative to the 10th Assembly of the World Council of Churches (WCC). This gathering took place between 30 October and 8 November, and the theme was 'God of life, lead us to justice and peace'.

The assembly brought together five thousand people from one hundred and ten countries – the sheer extent of the mix of people and the sense of vastness of the Christian community were extraordinary. It was a joy to be among so many people of faith. To worship, study and debate with others from around the world was encouraging and inspiring. Every morning we prayed the Lord's Prayer, each in our native tongue – a holy moment of inspiration.

The worship celebrated diverse traditions; it included litanies and songs from Africa, Asia, the Caribbean, Europe, Latin America, the Middle East, North America and the Pacific. I found the African and South American songs made my feet tap and were good for the soul. The Taizé refrains were movingly reflective. Morning worship was a wonderful window into the worldwide Church – revealing a wider vision of the Church than I had ever experienced. To discover Jesus in the other took on a whole new meaning.

Becoming aware of the frustrations of people living and praying in difficult places helped bring a perspective to our own fractured community. I found it inspiring and challenging to speak with Archbishop Thabo Makgoba about how South Africa's journey to peace has involved victims telling their stories as an essential element – an issue that still haunts us in Northern Ireland and as yet remains unresolved.

It is almost impossible to go anywhere in the world and not find an Irish connection. Archbishop Diarmuid Martin, the Roman Catholic Archbishop of Dublin, was a guest of the assembly. His reflections to the assembly were incisive and affirming, spoken with some Irish humour. He was the outgoing co-moderator of the joint working group for relations between the Roman Catholic Church and the WCC. The WCC does have a fascination with working groups, committees and structures!

The assembly was also disturbing as we heard of injustices throughout the world. To hear first-hand accounts of the deep divisions caused by culture, religion and wealth left us all having to examine our own prejudices and silence on such important matters. There was also the reminder of the reality of poverty, lack of education and lack of appropriate health care. The world's resources are unevenly divided and millions of people have no voice to change their circumstances. It was excruciating to hear from people caught up in war and civil unrest – stories that reminded us all of the worst that humans can do to each other. These accounts were from Christians living in the middle of the chaos and suffering of the world. We in Northern Ireland have many such stories that need to be heard.

There were numerous presentations and we discussed a vast number of topics. Churches worldwide were represented and the wealth of experience from so many different contexts was very stimulating. One comment from a nineteen-year-old girl from Malawi who is HIV-positive received a standing ovation, and will stay with me forever: 'HIV/Aids is not a punishment from God; it is a disease.'

It was a wonderful experience. I realised that the journey of unity is something we choose to make or not make. It is God's gift, but in Busan I met people who were committed to this journey and they deliberately sought to find Jesus in the other. If we do not think unity is important, it is easy to focus on the issues that we disagree on, and doing so pushes us further apart.

So often our disagreements are rooted in our different cultural backgrounds and upbringings. We make assumptions about the other and fail to get past our prejudice. The scriptures are an amazing gift to all disciples, but our interpretation of them can hinder us from hearing other viewpoints and interpretations. Eugene Peterson spent all his life in ministry, studying and teaching the scriptures. I find the following words he wrote in his journal illuminating: 'The Bible is inspired and absolutely reliable, Holy Spirit-given, protected and interpreted – so I can relax. That gives me a lot of freedom. I don't need to be overly cautious and nitpick. I work out of the entire canon of scripture, letting imagination be formed by everything there. Then prayerfully let myself go – wandering, connecting, remembering, whatever.'[3]

As I returned from Busan, I found myself inspired to renew my own commitment to work and prayer, that we might walk and live in the unity that Christ has given to his people.

Let me return to home and my friendship with Bishop Noël Treanor. We had various meetings over breakfast, lunch or coffee, when we continued to think and talk about what we could do together. There was an annual day visit to the Northern Ireland Hospice on Somerton Road, Belfast. This proved to be humbling as we met inspirational people facing very difficult journeys with cancer. We also attended many special services in different settings; worshipping together was an important statement of our unity in Jesus.

The suspicion and hurt across our communities has to be acknowledged. Unless we continue to listen to – and hear – each other, the divisions will deepen and be passed on to future generations. The work of listening is difficult and demands patience. There must also be the willingness to hear difficult and different views from our own. This is hard work! We must surely begin, as disciples of Jesus, to model this. We have been guilty of furthering division in our inability to move beyond our prejudices and assumptions. In my journey of discovering Jesus in the other, I have been enriched, challenged and blessed. I have been forced to understand my own faith and articulate it in ways that enable it to be heard. It has also been enriching to hear how other people have discovered ways of finding God's grace in their lives.

In every diocese in the Church of Ireland there is an annual diocesan synod. Essentially, this is our annual general meeting where we report on what has happened through our various committees and ministries. There are always ecumenical guests and Bishop Noël was a regular visitor – although I am not sure our visitors find it a stimulating event! Over the years in the Connor diocese we have also sought to introduce new voices, ideas and imaginative thinking. To facilitate this, we finish our diocesan reports in the afternoon and keep the evening free for a guest speaker.

On Thursday, 29 September 2016, we welcomed Archbishop Eamon Martin to address our evening session at the diocesan synod. He spoke about reimagining the role of the Church in our present culture. He challenged us not to do more for the existing members of our community, but 'to leave them there and go out to the margins'. There is also the need to evaluate our parish structures and the way we do things in the light of mission. During the evening Bishop Noël also addressed the synod, and at the end of the evening Archbishop Eamon took questions from the floor. Throughout his address and questions he spoke with humour and humility. It was an inspirational evening.

When we hear someone from a different church background and culture speak, it can be very helpful. To discover that he and the Church he served were facing the same issues as we were, to realise that we could learn from and support each other rather than compete, was very encouraging. To listen to someone who represents the 'other' and realise we are talking the same language, but with different nuances or emphases, is inspiring. At the heart of his address was the challenge for us to be disciples and to share the love and mercy of God with others.

I found leadership and ministry very demanding. There was loneliness in being a bishop that I had not expected. As an introvert, I found the constant being with people exhausting. I do love people, but I receive my energy from being on my own, and hence being with people all the time can be very draining. After eleven years as a bishop, I recognised the need to recover and be refreshed. With the support of the diocese and my fellow bishops, I planned a sabbatical for 2018. This would be three months to rest, study, write, travel and pray. When it arrived I was thrilled to have time to recover my inner quiet. My aim was to refresh my inner life and faith journey with Jesus.

I returned to work revitalised and was able to write about one of my favourite subjects, the incarnation. When Jesus was in the world he did not fix it, but he brought blessing to the hurting and broken. He challenged religiosity and helped us discover what God looks like in human form. He lived in our mess to help us live there too, knowing his presence and peace.

However, my return to work was quickly followed by a visit to my doctor, as I was having difficulty passing water. My blood results were alarming, showing a very high level of PSA (prostate-specific antigen). I was red-flagged to the City Hospital and very quickly discovered I had advanced prostate cancer. This meant the cancer had spread and needed urgent action. Within a month, I was on sick leave and faced a year of intensive treatment. I will record the rest of that journey in my next chapter, but suffice to say I was overwhelmed by love and prayers. It was particularly gratifying to receive so many prayers from those who, in our religious world of Northern Ireland, would be from the other side of the community!

I was now living in the mess of an uncertain journey and discovering the world of an unwelcome guest – cancer.

JIM > The Pain of Separation

I remember it more in emotions than in detailed facts. However, the facts are important too. I had come to the little Church of Ireland church over my lunchtime break to visit an installation inspired by the Lord's Prayer and reflecting the journey we had made in Northern Ireland through what we called, euphemistically and in the most horribly minimising way, the Troubles. I remember that the installation was physically very striking and emotive. I prayed my way round the stop-off points of the installation, each with items that spoke into the Lord's Prayer and our recent history. These included items symbolic of experiences and traditions from outside my own section of our community (I try not to talk about the 'communities' here, preferring to believe that we are one community that sectarianism has sectored). I paused and took in my situation. I was standing in a church from a different tradition, praying with items that drew me into considering suffering and sacrifice, again from outside my tradition and my own personal experience. It struck me as an important, rich and somewhat unusual position for me to be in. In fact, I remember smiling at where God was leading me on my faith journey. As I smiled, I realised that I felt at home here.

The minister, a friend of mine from the committee of the 4 Corners Festival (more of that soon), asked me to stay for the Eucharist service she was about to conduct. I agreed. There were five other people in the quiet church and we settled into our seats to pray and worship together. Again I felt at home in the service; even though the words were not altogether familiar to me, the rhythm of call and response, aided by a missal to direct me, drew me in. However, the comfort was to come to an end abruptly as I realised that the time was coming for people to go forward to the minister and receive communion. A flood of thoughts and emotions went through my head. They became an internal debate:

Just go and receive.

You are not allowed.

You are welcome here and the minister will happily give you the Eucharist.

I know, but as a Catholic I am not meant to.

No one will know.

There's no integrity in that.

You will hurt her feelings.

That's a low blow.

It's the truth.

I know. This hurts.

Hurt. That is the overriding emotion of this whole memory. I didn't receive communion. Instead, I presented myself for a blessing. My friend gave me her blessing and the service went on.

After the service, my friend came to me. I think I saw hurt in her eyes. But that's maybe a projection of my own hurt that I have attributed to her in my memory. She told me that I would have been welcome to receive. I told her that I knew and appreciated that. However, it was my own tradition's rule that we as Catholics do not receive the Eucharist outside of the Catholic Church. This wise woman nodded and then smiled at me.

'I know, I know. But, Jim?'

'Yes?'

'Did you see the other four people with us?'

'Yes.'

'Two of them are Catholic people from the local parish.'

Wow, this was a complex interaction! We had a brief discussion about how we longed for a time when these sorts of situations did not arise, before I bid her farewell and took my leave.

I walked out of the dimly lit, quiet oasis of the church into a bright spring day, with traffic busying past in both directions. I felt torn. Part of me wanted to join the hustle and bustle and get back into the day. Another part of me was still inside the church, trying to work out what had just happened. In some way, the pain of the experience summed up something of the separation of our community at large, during and after the conflict and peacemaking.

I also felt a little bemused. How did this Catholic boy from what was essentially an enclave end up in this situation anyhow? How is it that I ended up with this woman, a minister in the Church of Ireland, as a good friend? Well, for that story we need to go back a little bit in time.

Having taken up my post with the Living Church Office in 2012, one of the first tasks I got my teeth into, along with my colleagues Alan McGuckian and Paula McKeown, was planning for and holding a great gathering of people from across the Catholic Diocese of Down and Connor in the Waterfront Hall in Belfast in September 2013. It was to be called a congress and we worked for a full year on developing parish ministries, particularly parish pastoral councils, enlivening and encouraging parish communities and endeavouring to put together a vibrant and celebratory gathering for those attending. Boy, it was hard work!

One of the highlights of the congress was to be the inclusion of Bishop Alan Abernethy, then Bishop of the Diocese of Connor, as a guest of Bishop Noël Treanor, then Bishop of Down and Connor, and as a speaker on the theme of reconciliation. At the Living Church Office we became convinced that we could play a part in some small way in terms of peace-building and opening up conversations with those from other traditions. In particular, Alan McGuckian, then a Jesuit priest, now a bishop in the Raphoe diocese, had some experience in inter-church dialogue. In this regard, and in many others, Alan McGuckian was a mentor to me.

One of my areas of work was in the development of parish pastoral councils, meaning that I was often out travelling around parish communities in the evenings. As the time came close for the congress in Waterfront Hall, I took the opportunity to promote it whenever I was out in the parishes. I remember one night a man stood up and lambasted me for promoting a gathering where a Protestant had been invited to speak! Well, before I could say anything the local priest replied in no uncertain terms that this man was wrong in what he was saying and not only was Bishop Alan welcome to come to the congress, he would be a valuable contributor. The other people there burst into a round of applause. There was no further comment from our initial contributor.

Bishop Alan's involvement did cause quite a stir, though. It was noted as a progressive and encouraging moment for the vast majority of people who attended the congress. His involvement caused a stir in me, too. It was the first time I had met Alan, although because of the heavy workload on the day, we didn't get to spend a lot of time together. I remember feeling that the Holy Spirit was at work in him and in his involvement with us.

Our paths crossed again soon after the congress when, on the back of his involvement, one of his joint Church of Ireland/ Methodist communities on the outskirts of Belfast asked me to come and work with them on a piece of pastoral planning. This was the first time I had worked in this way with a group of people from the Protestant tradition. I wondered how it would go. Would my approach to prayerful discernment of our plans go down well? Would I be accepted as someone with something to offer? Looking back, I find it funny to see just how nervous I was. So nervous, in fact, that I turned up one hour earlier than I was meant to for our first session.

When we began, I soon realised that the work would go well. We prayed beautifully together. The insights the group brought to the scripture piece I had introduced for our prayer time were honest, searching and helpful. I believe we planted seeds of a good relationship in how we prayed together. That is a lesson I have taken with me ever since.

Not only did this piece of work go well, but it was indeed the start of a relationship that lasts to this day. I have been invited back to church services, to exhibitions and prayer breakfasts for nearly ten years now. It was due to one such invitation that I got to meet Bishop Alan again, at an exhibition of art inspired by the cross of Jesus. Meeting again after the congress was a joyful affair. I remember he greeted me with 'Brother!' and a hug. Thank God, I have heard that exclamation and felt that hug many times since.

It is hard to underestimate the impact of having the relationship with that Church of Ireland/Methodist community. Being made to feel welcome – even more, being made to feel part of the community – blasted away any remaining sense of the myth of otherness I had left in me. Sure, we had differences – some big differences – in our outlook on theology, politics and nationality. But I found we shared a common core. That core was our humanity and our belief that we were all created by God, and therefore somehow sisters and brothers, just as Bishop Alan had exclaimed.

It was around this time that I was invited to join the committee of the 4 Corners Festival. The 4 Corners, as we know it in shorthand, is an inter-church arts festival sited in, and reflecting on, the city of Belfast, Northern Ireland. Incorporating a wide variety of artistic practices, the festival always has an eye to peace and reconciliation and building God's kingdom in the city and beyond.

Itself a product of an unlikely, yet deeply blessed, friendship between Father Martin Magill, a Catholic priest, and the Reverend Steve Stockman, a Presbyterian minister, the 4 Corners has been a vehicle for making friends and building relationships across the wounded and wonderful city of Belfast and beyond. There is a certain spirituality that comes with the 4 Corners. It is a spirituality of curiosity in the 'other', a spirituality of willingness to move out of our own 'corner' (physically, emotionally and theologically), and a spirituality of acceptance that difference occurs but does not need to become division.

Over the years that I have been involved with the 4 Corners, I have met people from all over the world who come to visit the city of Belfast and take in the festival while they are here. My life has been enriched by the perspective of the very-often-bemused visitors when they hear about or witness our divisions. However, it is the contact with those who live here in the city I share with them that has impacted me most.

One such contact encapsulates almost my entire experience in this regard. First, let me return to the beginning. I was born in October 1971 in a small hospital in the Sandy Row district of South Belfast not long after the 'Troubles' (as they would become known) raged into life. My dad tells me that that on the night I was born, he made his way through burning barricades and street riots to get to the hospital and then back through the same barricades and riots to go out to 'wet the baby's head', as the saying goes here – in other words, to have a drink with family and friends to celebrate the arrival of his firstborn child. My mother spent a night or two in the hospital and then she went home, baby me in tow. Sandy Row is known as a Protestant, loyalist part of Belfast, and so over the years I very rarely visited the area. In fact, only in adulthood did I find out where the hospital, now used as a storage facility for the local Health Trust, is situated. At once, I have felt both connected to, and disconnected from, Sandy Row.

Imagine my surprise when, in 2020, another 4 Corners friend, the Reverend David Campton, a Methodist minister, asked if I would contribute a piece of music to the 125th anniversary service for Sandy Row Methodist Church. I was humbled. We were in the grip of the pandemic, with its resultant restrictions, and therefore the service was to be online via Zoom with a virtual cup of tea or coffee afterwards. As it turned out, I had been working on an original song that spoke about the importance of unity and community. I gladly accepted the invitation and set about recording the song. I will reproduce the words of the chorus here:

I am more than just me
You are more than just you
When we walk close to God
We know that it's true
That God calls us to stand
Together, we see
You are more than just you
I am more than just me.

The song is inspired by St Paul's desire that the communities he wrote to would 'preserve the unity of the Spirit by the peace that binds you together' (Eph 4:3) and, while I had written most of it before this invitation, it had never really been finished or found a home. It seems the song was waiting to get invited to Sandy Row!

Having my song played at the service and meeting with a group of Methodists from Sandy Row afterwards was an honour for me. In some way, it felt like I was tying together some threads from my past. I was returning to my birthplace. Having been born into violence and division, with myths of 'them' not being like 'us', here I was once again meeting and having tea and coffee with 'them', but it all felt like 'just us'.

That feeling of 'just us' has become a defining feeling as I have grown older. I don't apply it only to church or religions. I feel what Julian of Norwich in *Revelations of Divine Love* called a 'oneing' taking place – a coming together of all creation under God. I am becoming more and more convinced that God's plan for the world involves unity, rather than division.

Jesus exclaimed, 'that they all may be one, as you, Father, are in me, and I in you; that they also may be one in us, that the world may believe that you sent me' (Jn 17:21). 'Just us' has become a standpoint for me to take in life. There are no 'them ones', just us. And it was this 'just us' standpoint that took me into the little Church of Ireland church to visit my friend and her installation on the Lord's Prayer. It was this 'just us' standpoint that encouraged me to stay for the service and it was this 'just us' standpoint that caused me to hurt as I refused communion in favour of a blessing at that service.

While we have come a very long way here in Northern Ireland in breaking down barriers of all sorts over the years, many barriers to unity remain and some new ones have emerged. Coming from, and working primarily in, a Catholic context, I see that within my own tradition we are also burdened by a spirit of exclusion and disunity in some ways. Not only was I forbidden under my tradition to receive communion in my friend's Church of Ireland service, she who freely offered my full participation in her service would not have been graced with the same offer had she come to a Catholic Mass. We have put a lot of rules in place around who should and should not be offered the Eucharist at Mass. This does not simply apply to those of different Christian traditions. It applies to those deemed neither, in accordance with our belief that the Eucharist is the Real Presence of Christ, or those deemed unworthy due to sinful behaviour. This last one has garnered a lot of attention of recent years as it seems to have been applied almost exclusively according to judgements on sexual morality. We hear, for example, of LGBTQ couples being denied the Eucharist in some rare instances. We never hear of someone being denied the Eucharist for stealing from the poor or exploiting workers. I have a feeling that if we pressed pause in the church just before communion and really examined ourselves, we'd realise that no one is really more worthy than anyone else. I'm with Pope Francis when he says, 'The Eucharist, although it is the fullness of sacramental life, is not a prize for the perfect but a powerful medicine and nourishment for the weak'.[4]

I long for the day when we might see a way for Christians – indeed any person – to take part fully in each other's liturgies; liturgies that feed us, strengthen us and bring us together. And I long for us all to take that display of unity and to bring it into the world with us – God knows, we have a lot of divisive issues that the unifying love of God can heal.

REFLECTION

Alan and Jim have highlighted the following issues in this chapter:
1. The pain of separation and the joy of journeying together
2. The tension of Spirit versus Law in Church institutions
3. Eucharist, the meal of unity, has become a painful source of division

Reflect
In what ways do you see these challenges in your own life experience?

Challenge
Having read these reflections, in what ways do you hear God challenging you to discover Jesus in the other?

Pray
Matthew 23:23
Mark 14:22-24

NOTES

1. Eugene Peterson, *Christ Plays in Ten Thousand Places: A Conversation in Spiritual Theology*, Michigan: Eerdmans, 2005, p. 200.
2. Jean-Pierre de Caussade, *The Sacrament of the Present Moment* (trans. Kitty Muggeridge), San Francisco: Harper & Row, 1982, p. 99.
3. Collier, *A Burning in My Bones*, p. 276.
4. Pope Francis, *Evangelii Gaudium*, Vatican Press, 2013, 47.

CHAPTER EIGHT

Brokenness, Grace and Unity

ALAN > The Unwelcome Guest

The initial part of my cancer journey was surreal. We were in shock. As we talked and prayed, we were in a state of confusion, fear and uncertainty. There were many unanswered questions and it would be weeks before we had a full understanding of what we were facing. I know that Liz found this a torturous time; being a medical doctor, she was aware of the worst-case scenario. I also believe that on a cancer journey it is much harder for those watching and supporting, as all the attention is on the one with cancer.

The realisation came very quickly that we had to tell our children, Peter and Ruth. I spent some time imagining the telephone calls, planning what to say, but these two phone calls were incredibly difficult. It had to be by phone as our son lived in Cornwall and our daughter lived in Edinburgh. 'How on earth do you get your head around telling your children – of any age – that Mum or Dad has cancer?'[1] Their response was wonderful and the support of my family was unshakable, as it always has been. They have had their own journeys in dealing with my diagnosis and the ripples of cancer stretch far and wide.

The unanswered questions were constantly present. How bad is the tumour? Has it spread? What is the treatment? When can we get started? What about work? Who do we tell? When do we tell them? The list was endless and kept changing, and I will be forever grateful to Liz for her unending support when it was very difficult for her not to share her fears with me. We were haunted by fear in these initial few weeks. I understand and appreciate the analogy in the following words: 'Brain studies have shown that we may be hardwired to focus on problems at the expense of positive vision. The human brain wraps around fear and problems like Velcro. Conversely, positivity and gratitude and simple happiness slide away like cheese on hot Teflon.'[2]

Within a week of the blood test, I had my first hospital appointment. This was the beginning of my treatment journey. I was quickly given hormone injections to stop the tumour from growing and spreading. Scans and a biopsy soon followed. Having a biopsy of the prostate was uncomfortable, but not painful.

The CT scan had been carried out before the biopsy and I was given the results of the scan just after the biopsy. I fainted! The cancer had spread beyond the prostate into my pelvis, my ribs and some lymph nodes. We were in shock; it was not what we had hoped for. The good news was that it had not spread any further and the tumour was not as aggressive as it might have been.

The first meeting with my oncologist was very upbeat and positive. The initial plan was for six sessions of chemotherapy followed by radiotherapy. It was obvious that I could not continue to work through my treatment and I had no choice but to go public with my news. I wanted to tell people what was happening rather than have people guessing or making assumptions. There was a period of six weeks between the original diagnosis and my having to stop work.

My journey with cancer became very public once I told the diocese and the wider Church. However, the response was amazing; the letters, emails, phone calls and expressions of love and support were humbling. I received many Mass cards assuring me of the prayers of many, many people.

I had one session of chemotherapy every three weeks, with a four-week break at Christmas when, with my oncologist's support and encouragement, we had a family holiday. I was physically very tired, but the stimulus and joy of being with family helped me enormously. My consultant until this point was Aidan Cole, with whom I had formed a rapport. It was just before my fifth session that he told me I was going to be invited to join a clinical trial. I was introduced to Professor Joe O'Sullivan, who explained what the trial would entail. It would involve finishing my chemo sessions and then having thirty-seven radiotherapy treatments (rather than twenty). Then there would be six injections of radium-223, as part of an 'AdRad' trial based in the Cancer Centre at the City Hospital. These monthly injections were a bone-seeking missile to attack the bones where the cancer had spread. The aim of the trial was to test how all these forms of treatment would work together. It was not a cure, but certainly allowed the prospect of a longer survival time. I signed up and a new part of this strange journey unfolded.

Throughout it all I was impressed, encouraged and inspired by the staff and patients I encountered. I have sometimes read newspaper reports and listened to television or radio news that has blamed the health service for all sorts of problems. There have been mistakes, but every day in our hospitals and health centres hundreds of people are helped and cared for by an amazing array of people with different skills and talents. They are so often taken for granted and criticised. I want to record my thanks for the level of care and support I received from so many who were simply doing their job. Thank you!

Radiotherapy was the next stage of the journey and was a daily experience, Monday to Friday, for thirty-seven days. For those being treated for prostate cancer there was a simple mantra: 'Empty the bowel and fill the bladder.' This was to ensure that vital organs were not damaged by the radiation. Without discussing this in too much detail, suffice it to say when the bladder was full, my hope was I would be taken on time!

It was while I was having this daily treatment that I met another Joe. He was from a Roman Catholic background and we shared a great deal during our daily wait for treatment. We were fellow travellers in the clinical trial. Sharing our life stories and how faith played a crucial part for us both was enriching. His love of church, daily worship and the sacrament was an encouragement. His self-effacing faith, which was deep, personal and rooted in practice, was an inspiration. He will be embarrassed reading these few words, but he was a wonderful blessing to me as we journeyed with cancer.

It has always been a privilege to share with people as they asked for prayer and support through illness, bereavement or the daily grind of living. Pastoral ministry is what we offer each other as fellow disciples. As part of my call to ordination, this essential pastoral ministry was something I always felt compelled to offer to others. When Liz and I began to face into the future with the reality of a cancer diagnosis, we wanted someone to journey with us and to pray with us.

I have known and respected Canon David Jardine for many years. He was passionate about the healing ministry of Jesus offered to us through our fellow disciples. Brother David lived close to us and we invited him to pray at regular intervals. The evening before each of my six chemo sessions, he spent a short time reading a psalm and a short scripture passage. He then anointed us and prayed with us. These were holy moments that brought us deep peace and joy. It was very clear to us both that Jesus was present with us on this unwelcome journey with cancer. Brother David continued to pray with us throughout my treatment plan and we will be forever grateful to him for his ministry of prayer and help.

It was now over twelve months from the blood test results until my final proton injection, followed by more scans and blood tests. Then we went to see Professor Joe to discover the results. It was a wonderful moment when I realised that, thanks to the treatment, the scan before and the scan after showed very different results. I still had cancer, but it was no longer spreading and it was not showing in my bones. I describe this as a miracle of modern medicine.

There was relief, joy and exhaustion. It had been a long, difficult but rewarding journey. I am incredibly grateful for the wonderful care of our health service. It is hard to overstate the dedication and clinical expertise of those involved in cancer research and clinical trials. Within our own community we have people who seek every day to alleviate the pain and suffering caused by cancer. I salute them and hope we will all find ways of supporting and helping the fight against cancer.

Recovery became my main focus at this point and yet I also had to prepare for retirement. However, before I discuss that part of the journey I want to mention someone else whose path crossed with mine on numerous occasions during the last few years of my ministry as a bishop, and who shaped those years. He was the faithful and dedicated MP and MLA (Member of the Legislative Assembly) for South Belfast, Dr Alisdair McDonnell. He came from a different tradition and worshipped in a different church, but I found his passion for social justice inspiring. While religious institutions can often be detached from the everyday hardship and struggles of poverty faced by many, he was committed to making people's lives better no matter which community they came from.

He invited me to join him and others on a newly established board of trustees. The Goliath Trust, which raises funds to help address the persistent problem of educational underachievement in Northern Ireland's most disadvantaged areas, was established in August 2017. Its focus is providing targeted financial support to schools that are most in need. I have found the work and energy of this board an inspiration, a board that represented the vision and dream of a man of faith – a faith that meant he had to help others in need and use his drive and energy to bring others with him. This is a board I am proud to serve on in retirement as it seeks to make a difference with practical and focused help.

The decision to retire was a difficult one to reach, but I did not really have any choice, as with ongoing medication and its side effects I knew I would not have the energy needed to continue as bishop. It is a demanding, exciting, but draining role, and for the sake of the diocese, my family and my own well-being, retirement was the only option.

There were various procedures to follow and medical assessments to attend. The end result was that I was to retire on 31 December 2019. A farewell service to be attended by representatives from the parishes in the diocese was arranged for Thursday, 19 December in St Patrick's, Ballymena. This was a service that I planned and put together.

It was an emotional evening, but I was delighted to choose the hymns and readings and to preach myself. I was also able to invite friends who had journeyed with me from different traditions and who had helped me discover Jesus in the other. Some of them took part in the service and it was a joy to have Brother Eric and Brother Mark from Holy Cross Abbey, Rostrevor, sing a psalm. They had done the same at my ordination as a bishop in 2007. Bishop Noël also processed with me as we began the service. Other denominations were represented by people who had become friends and fellow disciples: Bishop Sarah Groves of the Moravian Church; Charles McMullen, a former Moderator of the Presbyterian Church in Ireland and minister of the local church in Bangor, where we were going to live; and Heather Morris, secretary of the Methodist Church in Ireland. One of the roles I had as a member of the Church of Ireland was to be co-chair of the Church of Ireland and Methodist Covenant Council, and Heather was the Methodist co-chair. This was an enriching experience and it was facilitating closer unity between these two denominations.

I preached on that beautiful verse in St John 12:21: 'We want to see Jesus. Can you help us?' As we prepared for retirement we had to declutter. We were moving to a very small house compared with the space in the bishop's residence. Various charity shops were visited many times and I gave most of my books away to people who would use them. It was helpful for us to consider what we had as we gave so much away. Decluttering helped us focus on the essentials, just as this scripture helps us focus on what matters: seeing Jesus.

Reflecting in the sermon on my years as a bishop, I shared some of the lessons I had learned. We have too many church buildings and they become a millstone around our necks. They are financially and emotionally draining and can be the source of unhelpful conflict. There is an over-dependence on clergy. Within my own tradition we have been very faithful in baptising, marrying and burying, but have failed to take seriously the command to make disciples. The focus on clergy being and doing the ministry has meant that many people have not been given the opportunity to minister and develop their gifts and talents. The focus on clergy has also meant that Sunday worship has focused on what we do inside the building rather than how we serve our local communities outside it.

Ministry and mission are always meaningful when we can perform them together with Christians from different denominations. One of the great joys of ministry, as I have experienced it, is that of working and serving with people from other Christian traditions and in so doing discovering Jesus in the other. The kingdom of God is much more important than our individual denominations.

I can identify with the sentiments of Eugene Peterson: 'Having grown up in a sectarian world, where everyone outside the Pentecostal sphere was viewed with suspicion, Eugene found it eye popping to brush up against Presbyterians and Baptists and Catholics and Methodists. "But the disconcerting thing", he wrote in an article a few years after college, "was … that they were better Christians than I was."[3]

Two weeks after the farewell service in Ballymena, we moved house and the new state of retirement began. It was a difficult transition as it was forced upon me by the uncertainty of my long-term health, but slowly, with time and the love of family and friends, retirement has become a gift to be enjoyed. I made a promise to my family and myself that I would not take on any new dates for six months.

I broke that promise, however, even before I retired. The invitation to speak during the inter-church 4 Corners Festival, co-founded by the Reverend Steve Stockman and Father Martin Magill (a Presbyterian minister and a Roman Catholic priest), was impossible to refuse. The theme was 'Building a City of Grace'. I was invited to speak at St Anthony's Catholic Church in the Willowfield area of East Belfast in early February.

It was an honour to be invited, and this invitation allowed me to revisit some seminal moments on my journey of faith. It facilitated a return to my teenage years and the night I witnessed a crowd of rioters desecrate St Anthony's. That was a moment that changed my life forever. To be asked to speak there, nearly fifty years later, was a moment of special grace.

It was a joy to have Bishop Noël and Jim Deeds there in St Anthony's to support me with their friendship. It was an additional blessing that my fellow speaker was Brendan McAlllister, who had played such a formative role in my journey with Jesus when I was a student in Queen's. It was a wonderful evening: I met some old neighbours and people who remembered that night of desecration and the response of grace from some Protestant neighbours who arrived to help in the tidy-up operation.

Brendan was subsequently ordained a permanent deacon. Tragically, he died very suddenly after a short illness in December 2022. May he rest in peace and rise in glory.

The essence of this journey for me has been the relationships and friendships with people who are from different backgrounds and church affiliations, and there is such joy when the Spirit enables us to see the richness of each other in Jesus. My prayer is that many fellow disciples will continue to know the joy of discovering Jesus in the other and help bring healing and grace where there is deep hurt and suspicion. The mindset of suspicion and mistrust, of seeing danger instead of difference, must be challenged. Within the world of Christendom we must stop labelling and judging each other and thereby refusing to engage with those we differ from. It is critical that we take seriously the prayer of Jesus, to live out our unity, which is his gift to us all.

> It is only if we realize this that our world can really change because it is only then that liberals and conservatives, pro-life and pro-choice, Catholics and Protestants, Jews and Arabs, Arabs and Christians, black people and white people, men and women, and people wounded in different ways can begin to stop demonizing each other, begin to reach across to each other, begin to feel sympathy for each other, and begin, together, to build for a common good beyond our wounds and differences.[4]

JIM > An Unwelcome but Familiar Visitor

Constant doing. Constant proving, perhaps, that I was worthy of the role. Constant working. These are not the elements of a healthy life. They were, however, the elements of the life I was living. And so it was, in the late autumn of 2018, that I became ill. Following on from my decision earlier that year not to continue training as a deacon, I had thrown myself into hard work even more than before. I was working twenty-five- or thirty-day stretches without a day off. While I could not see it, I was becoming unwell. I woke up one morning and said to my wife, Nuala, 'I can't go in to work today.' I broke down. My body was tired. But much more, and much worse, my soul was tired.

In the previous days there had been a murder at the gates of the school where I had gone as a teenager. A man who was waiting for his son to come out of school was shot nine times in front of other schoolchildren and teachers, who fought to save his life but to no avail. I remember having been disgusted by the killing that had once more visited my community. As happens so often in traumatised communities such as ours, one tragedy awakens the memories of other tragedies. Already tired and emotionally fragile, I felt the sorrow of this man's family and saw the mess it left behind in the school communities as they struggled to make sense of the senseless. I remembered my own losses, too: the people close to me who had died, albeit in less violent ways. I remembered the days of my childhood, growing up with fear and anxiety in times marked by conflict. One such memory comes back to me from the early 1980s.

'Hey, look. It's a hand grenade.'

'Where?'

'Here, in the hedge.'

A gaggle of us nine-year-old boys, eyes like flying saucers, crowded round a gap in a hedge at the bottom of our street.

A moment before, we had been playing football. Someone had gone for a goal, overshooting by a few feet and leaving the ball stuck in the hedge of the house beside our imaginary goal posts – in reality, a gap between houses leading to the entry that ran the length of the street. Sticking to the golden rule of 'he who hits it goes and gets it', the wayward shooter ran over to the hedge to retrieve the ball. It was he who made the discovery.

Standing in the street with my friends, looking into the gap in the hedge, I could see a green oblong object with knobbly bits jutting out and furrows between. Familiar with Second World War movies and toys as we all were, we recognised the shape immediately – an Allied Forces hand grenade. Its butt end was raised up and pointing towards us with its top end obscured by being stuck in the ground at the base of the hedge.

'Is it real?'

'I don't know, I've never seen one.'

'It's small, isn't it?'

'Lift it up.'

'You lift it up.'

'Chicken. Buk, buk buk.'

'No, I'm not.'

'Lift it, well.'

So the conversation went between us with no one ever likely to reach in and grab the thing.

Our gathering round the hedge caught the attention of an adult walking up the street.

'What are you boys doing?'

'Missus, there's a hand grenade in this hedge.'

'Jesus, Mary and Joseph!' This was and is the universal prayer uttered by all old women in West Belfast from time immemorial and that day it came with an admonishment:

'What the hell are youse doing standing so close to it?! 'Mon away ah that.'

She ushered us away and made us promise not to go near the hedge. We promised and she went off to get other adults. Soon, there was a right old crowd standing a few yards back from the hedge, wondering what to do.

One of those who gathered was my father.

After a few minutes of different people offering different opinions, I saw my father come away from the crowd and go over to the hedge. He told everyone to stay back. We did.

He went right over to the spot where we had found the offending object and took a look. For my young boy's eyes this presented a confusing picture. I didn't know how to feel about what I saw. I was part petrified and part proud of the old man (the old man would have been about thirty-seven at the time; not old at all to this old man now!). I saw him lean in very close, until his head was inside the growth of the hedge. Everyone looked on with breath held. I remember the coldness of the fear that overtook me in that moment. It was like time had stood still and the air itself all around me was frozen. I held my breath. In fact, I think I was unable to breathe with the fear. He cocked his head, first this way and then that. And then from inside the hedge he said,

'No. It's not real.'

How he was so certain, we didn't know. But certain he was, because he reached in and lifted the grenade out.

'It's plastic. It's okay, it's plastic.'

After a moment of uncertainty, the people looking on walked over to my father to see. Indeed, the 'grenade' was actually not made of metal and explosives. It was made of plastic and sherbet. It was a hand-grenade-shaped sherbet holder – a sweet for children. I kid you not! In Northern Ireland. In the middle of the Troubles. A sweet in the shape of a hand grenade. You couldn't make it up.

It seems that a child had discarded the 'grenade' some time previously and the ball hitting the hedge had revealed it in its dirt- and leaf-covered resting place.

As quick as the drama began, the drama ended. The adults went back to their houses. We children did what all children do in the midst of conflict; we filed the trauma away and got on with life as best we could. Seeking a return to normality, we started our game once more as if nothing had happened.

'That shot took a deflection off you. It's our corner.'

'No, it didn't. You hit it wide. It's a goal kick.'

'Wise up, it's a corner.'

As the game resumed, so did life. Sadly, there were to be other times that real weapons did appear in and around the street I lived in. But for that day, no one got hurt. Nothing got damaged. It was a good day.

These memories, reawakened in 2018, became entwined with the events of violence I was witnessing in my community and, added to my exhaustion, my already fragile state of mind deteriorated further. Just as a pot of boiling water with the lid on is sure to spill over, so too my mind and emotions boiled over and the countless stretches of thirty-plus days working without a day off, followed by one or two days off before I got back 'in the saddle', took their toll. I was overwhelmed by grief, vicarious and personal, and by an anxiety the likes of which I had not felt before. Like a watch whose battery has run out of juice, I simply stopped; stopped in a heap.

Anxiety is my shadow. It is my unwelcome visitor, and while the anxiety I felt in autumn 2018 was of a magnitude I had not heretofore experienced, I had been bitten by anxiety before to the point that I had to take time out. Years before I made the move into pastoral ministry, I worked for the health service and, through a series of very stressful events, found myself needing to take time off work to heal. And, thank God, heal I did. As with all experiences in life, good and bad, that first bout of illness taught me many lessons. One of the lessons it taught me was how to heal. And, as with all valuable lessons, the learning took time and went through stages that I have found useful to reflect on since.

First, I went through a period of numbness, when my healing took the form of me giving myself permission to be sick. I had run away from my anxiety for months. I had fooled myself that I wasn't unwell and that I could 'work' myself out of exhaustion. How wrong I was! So that first stage involved allowing the wheels to come off; allowing myself to feel sad and disappointed; hurt and tired. During that time I relied on the merciful presence of family and good friends. Whether they knew it or not (and many did not and would have difficulty seeing themselves in this way), those kind, merciful people were the face of Christ to me. And they brought me a gentle word, a listening ear and an encouragement to see that things could and would get better. Letting go and allowing myself to be unwell also allowed my body and mind to consider the possibility of healing.

The next phase of the healing process for me involved what I call a 'reset'. This reset came in the form of getting back to something that I had been missing out on in the months previous – getting out of the house and into God's playground: nature. I find that walking, particularly in green spaces, gives me peace of mind. I had been stealing a walk here and there up until that point, but I hadn't been enjoying long walks with my mind only on the beauty around me. And so, in this second phase, I reset the balance and, rather than stealing a walk, I savoured a walk. Sometimes I walked for several hours in the parks and up the hills near my home. I regained perspective. I was so small in comparison with God's great work in nature. And if I was small, my problems were even smaller in comparison with God's ability to help me deal with them.

That led me to the third and most important stage of my healing. Now, it is important for me to note that I did not leave the previous two stages behind and move on without them. No. The compassion of family and friends as well as the consolation of the beauty of nature came with me, thank God. As I began to find strength, I found that I was drawn to go to Mass on a daily basis. I made the trip to the chapel each morning as part of my daily walk. I would go to Mass and then walk to the local park or up Divis Mountain, making sure I went back to the house to collect my faithful canine friend Jenny. Sadly, we lost Jenny in May 2022 at the grand old age of fifteen and a half. She accompanied me, silent witness to my healing, on all of those walks.

As well as going to church daily, I found that I reconnected to a prayer life that I had neglected in favour of putting most of my time and efforts into a busy work life. For me, that is never a good recipe. I began to read scripture more regularly. I spoke to God daily. I got the strength to put all of these stages of healing together and, over a period of several months, I healed to the point that I was able to go back to work. God is good.

God is good, but I am prone to making mistakes. And so, in the late autumn of 2018, my unwelcome, frequent guest came calling again, and this time with a vengeance. My insight, with the benefit of hindsight, allows me to see that I often feel a kind of imposter syndrome and use hard work as a way to cope with it. 'If I am working hard, then I must be the real deal' is something of how my thinking tends to go.

Imposter syndrome is something experienced by many lay people working in pastoral ministry in the Catholic tradition. In recognising the importance and giftedness of the ordained ministers, we have perhaps neglected to understand, recognise and esteem those lay people who offer their time, their lives, to minister to the people of God. I am so grateful that, as the years go on and as I continue to see the fruits of my work in pastoral ministry, I am able to put a narrative around my work that allows me to feel that God and, increasingly, the Church, sees and appreciates the work lay people do. That narrative will, please God, develop further as time goes on. However, back in the autumn of 2018, I had no such well-developed narrative and, once again, my unwelcome visitor caused the wheels to come off.

This time, though the anxiety was more severe, I was able to bring some of the lessons from previous bouts of anxiety to bear. In particular, I was able to reflect on the three stages of healing I had gone through those years before. It wasn't easy – for me or for

Nuala, who is such a source of strength, goodness and godliness for me. It took time, as all healing does. And knowing the three stages I would have to go through didn't mean that I could shortcut any of those stages. I remember having a conversation with my friend and companion on the road of faith and life, Father Brendan McManus SJ, just as I began to acknowledge that I was unwell. He held me in a loving and honest look and said, 'This is going to take months. You need to give it time.' Brendan is always a source of support in good times and in bad. And he knows what it means to face into suffering, difficulty and illness. I took his word and a word of wisdom from God. And I took time.

Being off work for a few months brought with it a gift. Isn't it a strange thing to reflect that in the midst of all sorts of difficulties in life we often find some gift or gifts to sustain us? Sometimes the gifts come in the shape of others, the people who support us. Sometimes they come in brief moments of respite or even laughter in the midst of sadness. For me, the gift came in stopping. Just stopping for a while. And in the stopping, I was able to go through the stages of healing I had experienced before and I was able to slowly begin again, again. Life is a series of new beginnings, isn't it? Often brought about by difficulty, we are given the grace to begin again, to learn and grow. I was blessed during those months at the end of 2018 and into 2019 to be able to reconnect to myself and to God in the love of my family and friends, in the beauty of the natural world around me, and in prayer.

I returned to work around February 2019 with a sense of inner strength and contentment I had not felt before. It is good for me to be grateful for that, even as I write these few words about that time. One unfortunate thing from that time was the fact that, due to being unwell, I was unable to contribute to or even attend the 4 Corners Festival, that great inter-church arts festival that has come to mean so much to me over this past decade and more.

Imagine, then, my absolute joy at being able to rejoin my colleagues in the organising committee to plan for the 2020 festival. I saw the festival that year as a personal milestone in my coming back from having been unwell. I wanted to throw myself into the consolation that bringing together people from all sorts of backgrounds and experiences gives those of us who facilitate such gatherings. And there was much consolation that year. From walking tours to music to drama to online night prayer, there was a vibrancy about the festival that matched the new life feeling I had been given by God over the months since getting better.

A high point of the festival for me was sitting in St Anthony's Parish Catholic Church in the Willowfield area of East Belfast listening to Bishop Alan Abernethy speak about his upbringing in this area (so beautifully recounted in the early chapters of this book). He spoke about how witnessing a violent crowd attack the church was a formative moment for him in understanding the futility of violence and the danger of the myth of 'otherness'. It resonated deeply with my own upbringing and the conclusions I have reached about the oneness of all people, despite any difference of religion, politics or other belief systems or identities. He spoke of the dark times of past violence and, as he did, I remembered that my own grandfather was one of the workers who had built the church we were sitting in. I remembered how he had told me about the violent opposition to the work they were doing to build a Catholic church where many people felt it was unwelcome in 'our area'. As I listened to this holy man – a Protestant bishop – speaking in that Catholic church, being welcomed by the local Catholic community, who were joined by so many people from other parts of the community, Catholics and Protestants alike, I could almost see my grandfather smile in my mind's eye. He passed on so much love to me; love that he had for all people. I think he would have been pleased that I was there. In some way I felt that I was representing him that night, and the good work he had done in building the church. It was a very moving experience.

Following the talk, we moved across the road from St Anthony's to Willowfield Church of Ireland Hall for refreshments. It was a chance to walk the walk as well as talk the talk. It was a chance to show that there are no boundaries that can keep people apart when we want to do the most natural of things – be friends.

My life is, please God, not over yet. It has been an interesting journey so far. As I grow older, I am graced to see the face of Jesus more and more often. It is not that Jesus is somehow more present. It is that God is willing me to co-operate with him in seeing clearly. God, give me eyes to discover Jesus in the other.

REFLECTION

Alan and Jim have highlighted the following issues in this chapter:
1. Our brokenness can be blessed by God
2. Moments of grace can be experienced in the midst of suffering
3. Unity is God's gift

Reflect
In what ways do you see these challenges in your own life experience?

Challenge
Having read these reflections, in what ways do you hear God challenging you to discover Jesus in the other?

Pray
John 17:20-23
John 4:4-30

NOTES

1. Deborah James, *F*** You Cancer: How to Face the Big C, Live Your Life and Still Be Yourself*, London: Vermilion, 2018, p. 118.
2. Richard Rohr, *The Universal Christ: How a Forgotten Reality Can Change Everything We See, Hope For and Believe*, London: SPCK, 2019, p. 63.
3. Collier, *A Burning in My Bones*, p. 46.
4. Ronald Rolheiser, *Our One Great Act of Fidelity: Waiting for Christ in the Eucharist*, New York: Image, 2011, p. 70.